NEW WORDS FOR OLD

RECYCLING OUR LANGUAGE
FOR THE MODERN WORLD

By the same author:

I Used to Know That
My Grammar and I (or should that be 'Me'?)
A Classical Education
An Apple a Day
Answers to Rhetorical Questions
Pushing the Envelope
The I Used to Know That Activity Book
Back to Basics
As Right as Rain
500 Words You Should Know

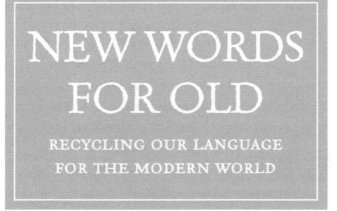

NEW WORDS FOR OLD

RECYCLING OUR LANGUAGE FOR THE MODERN WORLD

CAROLINE TAGGART

Michael O'Mara Books Limited

First published in Great Britain in 2015 by
Michael O'Mara Books Limited
9 Lion Yard
Tremadoc Road
London SW4 7NQ

A CIP catalogue record for this book is available from the British
Library.

Papers used by Michael O'Mara Books Limited are natural,
recyclable products made from wood grown in sustainable
forests. The manufacturing processes conform to the
environmental regulations of the country of origin.

ISBN: 978-1-78243-472-6 in hardback print format
ISBN: 978-1-78243-473-3 in e-book format

1 3 5 7 9 10 8 6 4 2

Designed and typeset by K.DESIGN, Winscombe, Somerset
Printed and bound by CPI Group (UK) Ltd, Croydon, CR0 4YY

www.mombooks.com

Contents

Introduction

The English language is a versatile thing, and we users of it can be agile too. When we invent new things, we are pretty good at coming up with names for them. *Aspirin, television, dot-com company* – there was a time when these things didn't exist, so there wasn't a word for them. There is now.

But sometimes when the need for a new word comes along we choose not to make one up; we simply adapt the meaning of an existing one, or put two together to form a third.

Modern life is full of such words, and that is what this book is about. It traces the development of GREEN from the days when it was only a colour, WEB when it was something spiders made and TROLLS when they were nothing more threatening than the bad guys in Scandinavian fairy tales. And it considers what happened when we put *advertisement* and *editorial*, *emotion* and *icon* and *modulator* and *demodulator* together to form an advertisement disguised as an editorial feature (ADVERTORIAL), an icon that helps convey the writer's feelings (EMOTICON) and a device that performs the dual functions of modulating and demodulating (MODEM). This sort of word, by the way, is called a *portmanteau*, an invention of Lewis Carroll's to describe a term that has two meanings packed into one.

The words discussed here aren't fancy ones that will improve your vocabulary and impress your friends – I'd be surprised if there were more than a handful that you don't use every day (though I have to confess that PRECARIAT and *emoji* were new to me). No, what I hope is interesting is the path that some very common words have followed in order to arrive at their present meanings. I find it intriguing, for example, that a SATELLITE used to be a person, that ROCK *and roll* got its name from the movement of a ship and that there was a time when you did your FILING by hanging things up on a piece of wire. I like the idea that a pedant would say it was impossible for a TRAIN to have only one carriage and that a CELL, whose purpose was once to keep people isolated, now enables you to keep in touch wherever you go.

Much of this book is about technology, an area that has developed – and continues to develop – so rapidly that it is in constant need of new vocabulary.

But again, much of that vocabulary isn't new at all: it's simply existing words given a new twist. We've had DISCS, DOMAINS, FORUMS and HARDWARE for hundreds, sometimes thousands of years. They were just *different* discs, domains, forums and hardware. In the future, words like this will almost certainly be adapted again and again to deal with advances as yet undreamed of.

That may sound like a daunting prospect, but I have no doubt that the English language will be able to cope. We have the old words – we just sometimes need to dust them off, polish them up and send them out with a clean handkerchief in their pockets, ready to face a bright new day.

Caroline Taggart
London, May 2015

CHAPTER ONE

Fun and Games

One of the main areas in which we've adopted words in the last hundred years or so is the entertainment business. This chapter looks at photography, the cinema, radio and television, but also at games, reading material and – for the benefit of those who see it as a leisure activity – shopping.

acoustic

As a branch of physics concerned with sound,
acoustics dates back as far as the seventeenth century,
when a record of the proceedings of the Royal Society
proposed the existence of three types of hearing
– direct, refracted and reflected, or, more technically,
acoustics, *diacoustics* and *catacoustics*. It seems
a shame that neither of the last two passed into
common use: a lot of fun could surely have been had
– and a lot of silly photos posted on Twitter – from a
misunderstanding of *catacoustics*.

No matter. *Acoustics* did catch on, both as a
science and as a description of the way sound was
transmitted in a building, particularly a concert hall.
Early sound recordings were made *acoustically* – that
is, using sound waves, which were collected in a horn
and channelled towards a thin diaphragm, causing
it to vibrate. These vibrations drove a stylus that
recorded the sound on a wax cylinder or DISC.

This method was superseded in the 1920s by
electric recording using a microphone. Then in due
course came the 1950s and the Fendo Stratocaster
– not the first electric guitar, but the one that really
made the idea take off. As electrical instruments
became the norm in ROCK 'n' roll bands, it was taken
for granted that a guitar was electric unless otherwise
specified: so the 'unplugged' guitar that had been

in use for centuries came to be called an *acoustic guitar* – one that relied on sound waves rather than electricity.

Much the same was true of pianos and various other instruments. The process is comparable to what is now happening with reading: the object that for hundreds of years we have called simply a *book* now needs to be designated a *print book* in order to distinguish it from the increasingly popular e-variety.

advertorial

A combination of *advertisement* and *editorial*, used to mean an advertisement feature presented as if it were a factual report, this modern-sounding word has in fact been around for a hundred years. It is found in 1918 in the works of the British publicist and author Charles Higham, who established the advertising agency that bore his name, and from the context it's clear that the concept, if not the term, had been known in the fledgling insurance companies that grew up in the London coffee houses of the seventeenth century.

A present-day New Zealand website advising on how to write a good *advertorial* suggests that you should use simple, everyday language and avoid slogans such as 'You've tried the rest, now try the best'; that you should tell a story rather than just fill the piece with facts; and that, although you should include your contact details, you shouldn't mention a price, as 'This tips the story too much towards the "advertisement" end of the scale.' I'm inclined to think that most readers know an advertisement when they read it and, if they don't, the words 'advertisement feature', which invariably heads the page, may give them a clue.

album

The Latin *albus* means 'white' and the neuter form *album* was used as a noun to describe a blank tablet, something on which you could write whatever you wanted. The sense of a blank book in which you or your friends could write messages or mementoes had emerged in English by the seventeenth century and the *photograph album* followed as soon as photography was sufficiently widespread for the expression to be needed. Thus the derivation of the word was obscured: the important thing about an album came to be not that it had started out as blank, but that it enabled you to build up a collection.

With the advent of recorded sound this new meaning became firmly established. In the 1920s, an *album of records* was a number of records on the same theme or by the same artist, sold as what today we would call a boxed set. This sense was largely abandoned after 1948, when the first 'long-player' was introduced by Columbia Records. Unlike the earlier '78s', which had a single song on each side, an LP could play for fifteen to twenty minutes a side and thus accommodate perhaps twelve songs on a single DISC. From being a collection of songs on a number of discs, therefore, an album evolved to be what it remains to this day – a collection of songs, usually by the same artist or from the same film, on a single record or, as FORMATS changed, a single CD or download.

biopic

A *biographical picture*, with 'picture' here meaning motion picture or movie, the *biopic* differs from the *docudrama* in that it tells the whole story of someone's life, rather than focusing on a particular incident. The concept is as old as cinema itself – the pioneering French film-maker Georges Méliès made a short biography of Joan of Arc in 1900. However, the website filmreference.com tells us that the biopic 'emerged as a recognizable subgenre in the 1930s' and that the first is generally considered to be the 1929 film *Disraeli*. Subjects ranging from Abraham Lincoln to Florence Nightingale soon followed, the only defining feature apparently being a resolute refusal to let the truth get in the way of a good story. 1940s biographies of composers, from Chopin to Cole Porter, were particularly notorious in this respect, though the paying public seems to have been willing to forgive most liberties if it got enough good tunes.

As for a *docudrama*, it's a cross between a *documentary* and a *drama*, reporting real-life events but using actors and probably fictionalizing some of the story for dramatic effect. The word dates back to the 1960s and in the cinema acclaimed films such as *All the President's Men*, *Argo* and *Selma* can be classed under this heading. On television, however, docudrama often mixes documentary techniques such as voiceover, a presenter talking to camera or news footage with the dramatization, producing an unhappy, 'between two stools' mix that suggests it's aimed at audiences who don't have the powers of concentration to take their documentaries straight.

See also MOCKUMENTARY.

blockbuster

A *block* in this context is a city block, the area bounded by two pairs of parallel streets – a common way of measuring distance in North America, where you are more likely to say, 'It's five blocks away' than 'It's ten minutes' walk.' This meaning of the word has been around since the late eighteenth century, with *bust* as a colloquial alternative to *break* only fractionally younger. The two were first put together during the Second World War, when a *blockbuster* meant a bomb capable of destroying a whole block. Once the war was over, the word quickly developed a figurative and more positive sense – to describe something as a *blockbuster of an idea*, for example, was to say that it was terrific, imaginative, breaking new ground.

Hollywood soon latched on to the term, applying it to 1950s films such as *Ben-Hur* or *The Ten Commandments* and then, over the decades, to *Cleopatra*, *Superman*, *Batman, Titanic, Avatar* and many others. The defining features of a *blockbuster movie* are massive production costs and huge marketing budgets, with perhaps less emphasis on the quality of the script or the acting (though the list I have given contains honourable exceptions to that stricture).

A *blockbuster novel* also tended to have a big marketing spend behind it; it was by definition long and usually broad in its scope, often covering several generations or continents, or describing a character's rise from grinding poverty to wealth beyond the dreams of anyone but a blockbuster novelist. Among the blockbusters of the 1970s and 1980s, written by the likes of Barbara Taylor Bradford and Shirley Conran, was a subgenre known as 'sex and shopping', to which in the late 1980s British writer Sue Limb brought a new twist. Under the pseudonym Dulcie Domum (which translates very roughly as 'the sweetness of home'), she wrote a column in the *Guardian* called 'Bad Housekeeping'; in it Dulcie is struggling to write a novel her spouse describes as a *bonkbuster*. Dulcie's description of the new gardener – 'stocky, balding Slav, with magnetic eyes and masterful manner with turnips' – gives an idea of the tone. Nobody who took their writing seriously would describe their work as a *bonkbuster*, but it has caught on among those who are dismissive of the genre and those who don't mind admitting that they are reading rubbish for the fun of it.

cameo

In the jewellery sense, a *cameo* is made from a precious or semi-precious stone, with two layers in different colours, carved so that the top layer – usually white or cream and often a head-and-shoulders portrait in profile – stands out from the lower one. Standing out is the point here: a *cameo part* in a play or film is a comparatively small role, often played by a famous actor, written so as to give that actor the chance to shine. Although *cameo* had been used to describe short literary sketches in the nineteenth century, the theatre and cinema sense didn't appear until the middle of the twentieth.

cartoon

The cartoons produced by Renaissance artists such as Raphael and Leonardo da Vinci weren't meant to make people laugh and didn't depict politicians with exaggerated facial features or wearing their underpants outside their trousers. Instead, they were full-size 'roughs', drawn on paper, whose designs would then be translated to canvas, tapestry, glass or some other medium – they were also often used to sketch the layouts of frescoes.

The first cartoon in the modern sense satirized this idea. Drawn by John Leech and entitled 'Substance and Shadow', it appeared in *Punch* magazine in 1843 and depicted London's poor visiting an art gallery. The accompanying editorial pointed out how ridiculous it was to expect the government to consider 'the wants of the pauper population, under the impression that it is as laudable to feed men as to shelter horses'.

The background to this is that the Palace of Westminster (home to the Houses of Parliament) had recently been destroyed by fire and was being rebuilt; some grand frescoes had been commissioned to decorate it and the preparatory cartoons (in the Leonardo sense) were exhibited to the public. *Punch*'s point was that, considering how many people were starving, the government might have found better things to do with its time and its money.

Punch had published full-page satirical drawings before and continued to do so, but now they had a new name – *cartoons*. And they began to evolve. The smaller (and funnier) 'gag cartoon', often occupying only a single column, developed over the next half-century and became a feature not only of *Punch* but later of the *New Yorker*. It is to a *Punch* cartoon that we owe the expression 'the curate's egg' ('parts of it are excellent'), while the *New Yorker* came up with 'back to the old drawing board'. It also famously published the image of a little girl whose mother is trying to persuade her to eat a newly fashionable vegetable, broccoli. 'I say it's spinach,' says the unimpressed child, 'and I say the hell with it.' You can't help wondering if Leonardo da Vinci, that well-known vegetarian, would have been amused.

chain

The thing about a *chain* is that it is made of distinct links, whether gold to hang round your neck or a cheaper but stronger metal to make a fence or a suit of armour. So although a chain forms a continuous, unbroken sequence, each link retains its own identity – it doesn't flow into its neighbour in such a way that you don't know where one ends and the other begins. The same applies to a *chain of mountains* – there's a lot of them, closely connected, but they are still individual peaks.

It's also true of a *chain of fast-food restaurants* or other businesses. Since the middle of the nineteenth century *chain* has been used to refer to a group of banks, theatres or shops under the same management. The question of individuality has, over the years, become rather a vexed one: the *chain* is now often compared unfavourably with an *independent*, with the implication that the range of goods and services on offer is likely to be more interesting and varied in the latter, and that the economies of scale that a chain can practise give it an unfair advantage. Moral and qualitative issues aside, the term *chain store* has been in existence – originally in the USA – since the early twentieth century.

Another realm where *chains* are used is that of tobacco: a hundred years ago a heavy smoker might be accused of smoking a *chain of cigarettes*: that is, one after the other, effectively without stopping. The term *chain-smoker* is older, having been borrowed from Germany in the 1890s and used there to describe Chancellor Otto van Bismarck, who apparently treated his cigars as if they were German states that needed to be unified.

channel

The point of a *channel* is that things flow through it. Etymologically it is related to *canal*, and in the early days what flowed through a channel was water; the word could also be used to refer to the water itself. The Brits have their own special one, of course, which – despite the efforts of tunnel engineers – keeps them obstinately separate from the continent of Europe.

As early as the sixteenth century, *channel* acquired a figurative sense: what passed through it was not water, but news and information. This later made it an ideal word to describe a specific aspect of a television service: it operated on a certain frequency (so, as with a watery channel, it couldn't flow around all over the place) and what came out of it was – sometimes – news and information. In this context *channel* originally referred to the waveband across which the programmes were broadcast, but very soon came to be used for the organization that did the broadcasting.

Modern DIGITAL and SATELLITE technology means that few television companies have to worry about wavelengths and frequencies any more, but the name persists.

draughts

Most meanings of the word *draught* are to do with pulling or drawing – a *draught horse*, for example, pulls a plough or vehicle, and *draught beer* is drawn from a barrel rather than kept in a bottle. In the fourteenth century a *draught* was a move in chess or similar games, referring to the action of drawing the piece across the board; a game that involved such a move was called *draughts* by about 1400, although something like it was played thousands of years ago in Mesopotamia and Egypt.

The American *draft* – taking people into the army – comes from the same root and derives from a sense that was in use in British English in the eighteenth century, a military unit 'drawn off' or detached from the main body and detailed to a specific duty.

Going back to board games, the word *chequer* or *checker* is connected with *chess* and originally designated the board and its pattern; from this comes *checkers*, the American name for what the British call draughts.

farce

The French word *farce* means stuffing, the savoury mixture you put inside roast poultry, and it comes from the verb *farcir*, to stuff or pad out. In the Middle Ages, extra words were sometimes inserted into religious chants to pad out the lines, and comic interludes were added to religious plays (surely a very early incidence of dumbing down): both were known as *farces*. By the sixteenth century, *farces* could be stand-alone comical works, and by the seventeenth the word was being used in non-dramatic contexts: *a farcical situation* could arise in the home or, to pick a random example, the Houses of Parliament, as easily as it could in the theatre.

jigsaw

The original *jig saw* was a narrow-bladed tool designed to cut intricate patterns in wood; etymologically it was connected with *jig* the dance and *jig* the jerky movement. By extension the term came to be applied to an elaborately decorative style of architecture and design (also known as fretwork) that could be executed by such a saw. The jig saw was known in the nineteenth century, but became more common after the Second World War, when a Swiss engineer installed a blade in place of a needle on his wife's sewing machine to enable him to work in wood. From this domestic application he developed a marketable saw and you can buy *jigsaws* (now normally spelled as one word or with a hyphen) in DIY shops the world over.

Precursors of modern *jigsaw puzzles* were known in the 1760s, when they were made of wood and represented maps that were used for the teaching of geography. The term itself, however, dates only from the beginning of the twentieth century, when the cardboard puzzles we know today became popular. By 1919 it was familiar enough for the explorer Ernest Shackleton to remark that Antarctic pack ice resembled 'a gigantic and interminable jigsaw-puzzle devised by nature'.

magazine

From the sixteenth to the early twentieth centuries a *magazine* was a storehouse or depot, in which you could store anything you liked – one early citation refers to 'lampes, oile, mats, and other necessaries'. As time went by, without losing this more general meaning, the word acquired the specialist sense of a store for ammunition, arms or explosives and, by the nineteenth century, the 'storage unit' on a repeating rifle or machine gun that fed cartridges into the breech of the gun. It was also used to refer to the goods themselves – the merchandise, ammunition or explosives that were stored in any of the various sorts of magazine.

Parallel to all this came the idea of a *magazine* as a book on a specific subject – a storehouse of information. The seventeenth and eighteenth centuries saw, among others, military magazines, the *Mariners Magazine* and the *Penmans Magazine*. We still have this sense in publications such as *Computing* magazine or *Cycling Weekly*. From these single-subject periodicals came the idea of a magazine on a *variety* of subjects, aimed at the general reader: as early as 1762 the satirist Oliver Goldsmith was able to write, 'It is the life and soul of a Magazine never to be long dull upon one subject.'

mall

The game of *pall mall* or *pell mell* was a bit like croquet, and was played on a long alley called a *mall*; this is how the London streets Pall Mall and The Mall got their names. When the game went out of fashion, Londoners adopted The Mall as a stylish promenade and from this the word spread across the world to describe any attractive avenue where the well-dressed could stroll. So when the concept of a *shopping mall* eventually came along, its defining feature was that it was pedestrianized.

Shopping malls take several forms – some are arcades, with a number of shops under one roof; others are more like shopping streets that are closed to traffic; still others are out-of-town agglomerations of shops with vast car parks. The arcade type is ancient – it existed in imperial Rome – but the modern pedestrianized *mall* came into being in the 1950s. Opinions vary as to which is the oldest, with Kalamazoo in Michigan, Appleton in Wisconsin and Bergen Park, New Jersey, all being contenders. But certainly the term *shopping mall* or just *mall*, used to make these havens of retail therapy sound glamorous, dates from this period.

mockumentary

This combination of *mock* and *documentary* means a spoof documentary, one that uses documentary techniques in order to satirize its subject. Although the word has been in use since at least the 1960s, it came into its own in the 1980s with the work of Christopher Guest, notably in the movie *This Is Spinal Tap*, which he wrote and starred in. This chronicles – or pretends to chronicle – life on the comeback tour of a heavy metal band and has the memorable, if meaningless, tag line 'Does for rock and roll what *The Sound of Music* did for hills'.

Documentary itself started life as an adjective, as in *documentary evidence* – the kind that is found in documents. This came to be applied to films or literary works based on fact and, from there, in the 1930s, became a noun meaning the film or literary work itself.

See also BIOPIC.

multiplex

The Latin suffix *-plex* is to do with plaiting or intertwining, and is often preceded by something indicating a number to produce a word meaning that number of things linked together. Thus a *duplex* is a two-storeyed house divided into apartments, one on each floor, and a *multiplex* is a cinema with several screens on the same site. The word has existed for hundreds of years in various scientific and mathematical contexts, where it means much the same as *multiple*, but it was adopted into cinema only in the 1970s.

Cineplex – a *cinema multiplex* – was the brainchild of the Canadian Cineplex Odeon Corporation, who opened the first such establishment in Toronto in 1979. There had been two-screen theatres since the 1940s and by the 1960s the occasional four- or six-screen one but, with eighteen screens and a seating capacity of 1,600, the Toronto Cineplex was in a different league.

patience

As a name for a family of card games, *patience* came into English from French in the early nineteenth century. According to card games expert David Parlett, playing cards on your own and concentrating on 'getting the game out' were once regarded as exercising the virtue of patience. (Nowadays, most people would say that it was, at best, a harmless way of passing the time and, at worst, a shameless waste of it.) Parlett also points out that in Italian *pazienza* can mean building card houses and that in French *patience* can be a JIGSAW puzzle, both of which require more patience and skill than a game that relies for its success on the random turning over of cards.

Less tricksome is the American *solitaire*, which derives ultimately from the Latin for *alone*. Before it became the name of various solo card games and the board game in which you jump one marble over another and aim to end up with just one left in the centre, it could mean a person who lived alone, or a precious stone set by itself, usually into a ring. The connection between all these senses is evident: you're on your own.

prequel

Sequi is the Latin for 'to follow' and it has spawned a number of English words, including *sequence*, *consequence* and *sequel.* A sequel is something that follows something else, usually a book, film or television series that was complete in itself, but was successful enough to justify another outing or to inspire another author. *Die Hard 2* and *Die Hard with a Vengeance* were sequels to *Die Hard*; P. D. James's

Death Comes to Pemberley was a sequel to Jane Austen's *Pride and Prejudice.* Both of these – and the various incarnations of *The Godfather*, *Rocky* and far too many others – told you what happened to the same characters later in their lives.

But, aha! thought somebody back in the 1950s. What if we want to know what happened to those characters *earlier* in their lives? Let's ignore the Latin origins, pretend that we think *se-* is a prefix and replace it with something that we know means 'before'. Lo and behold, the *prequel* was born. This decidedly unscholarly term is frequently applied to the trilogy of *Star Wars* films that begins with *The Phantom Menace*, released a decade and a half after the end of the first trilogy but dealing with earlier events; it's applied to the current television series *Better Call Saul*, which follows the career of the young Saul Goodman, a character previously seen in *Breaking Bad*; it's widely used in computer and video games, and it still makes purists shudder. The Urban Dictionary suggests that the logical development from an original followed by a prequel is a *postquel*; something that goes *between* existing episodes – some of the planned *Star Wars* films, for example – has even been referred to as an *interquel*; and I shudder to imagine how the purists are going to feel if either of those catches on.

quiz

The earliest (eighteenth-century) meaning of
this word is an odd or eccentric person or thing,
particularly someone whose appearance is
ridiculous: 'You look a complete *quiz* in that dress' or,
as an impudent Jane Austen character demands of his
mother, 'Where did you get that *quiz* of a hat?'
A *quiz* could also be a practical joke or joker. The verb
to quiz meant to tease, but also to look at closely, to
scrutinize (sometimes through a *quizzing glass* or
monocle) – and this idea of studying something and
summing it up may be the link between the early and
the modern meanings.

Only in the mid-nineteenth century did *quiz* take on
the sense of 'a set of questions used to test knowledge
or promote learning'; although this is now largely
an American usage, it was current in the UK in the
1950s and 1960s, and meant a short, impromptu test
at school that might happen at any time, as opposed
to the formal exams at the end of term. But by this
time it had also taken on the sense that is now most
frequent in British English, questions that you answer
for fun in a MAGAZINE or, increasingly of recent years,
in the pub.

simulcast

An amalgam of *broadcast* and *simultaneous*, a *simulcast* is a programme – usually either a concert or a sporting event – that is broadcast at the same time on television and radio, or on two or more television channels. It was coined in the US in 1948, when *The New York Times* recorded mournfully, 'A press agent at WCAU-TV in Philadelphia has rather timorously launched the verb "simulcast" into the uneasy seas of the English language.' In fact the concept goes back further than that, because Philadelphia had two simulcast radio stations, WCAU-FM and WCAU-AM, from 1941 until the mid-1960s. They apparently just kept quiet about this – or called it something else – for the first seven years.

sitcom

Short for *situation comedy*, a *sitcom* is a television comedy that gets its laughs from the situations in which the characters find themselves. The BBC's *Pinwright's Progress* (1946–7), forgotten by all but serious TV geeks, is credited as being the first such programme, the 'situation' being the ongoing conflict between two rival shop owners. But the term took off with the acclaimed 1950s American show *I Love Lucy,* in which the scatter-brained central character, played by Lucille Ball, got herself into a series of ridiculous situations. The pilot is summarized on IMDb.com as 'Ricky [Lucy's husband] tries to keep Lucy away from auditioning for a TV show, but when a clown becomes unavailable, Lucy takes his place', and it didn't get any less silly over the next six seasons. The term *situation comedy* was, of course, far too long to remain in common use and the abbreviated form was established by the early 1960s.

soap

The first *soap operas*, broadcast on radio in the USA from 1930, were so called because the sponsors who filled in the gaps between the bursts of drama were manufacturers of soap and detergents. This was daytime entertainment, aimed largely at housewives, to whom the products were supposed to appeal.

There were exceptions, of course. *Myrt and Marge,* launched in 1931, attracted the interest of chewing-gum supremo Wrigley and gave its lead characters the surnames Spear and Minter, to strengthen the association with its sponsor's top-selling flavour. But soapstuffs predominated and their name took hold:

the term *soap opera* was established by the end of the 1930s and had been abbreviated to *soap* by the 1940s.

From the beginning, *soaps* were characterized by sentimentality and melodrama, and it wasn't long before the expression was used of the wider world, not just radio entertainment. As early as 1944 a character in Raymond Chandler's thriller *The Lady in the Lake*, having poured out his woes about his ex-girlfriend, was able to say cynically, 'Thanks for listening to the soap opera,' confident that both his companion and the novel's readers would know what he meant.

spectacle

The Latin *spectare* means to look at, to watch, and by the fourteenth century in English a *spectacle* was something worth looking at, a public display, often a *spectacular* one. These senses are still current, though not always in a good way: *to make a spectacle of yourself* is to attract unwanted attention. But *spectacle* had another meaning, now obsolete – something that was made of glass and could be seen through. From this, as early as the fifteenth century, came the idea of a *spectacle* or *pair of spectacles*, which aided poor sight.

The word may not have come into being until then, but the concept of eyeglasses was almost a century older. The first known portrait of someone wearing reading glasses is part of a fresco of forty Dominican scholars commissioned from the artist Tommaso da Modena in 1352: the biblical commentator Hugues de Provence (also known as Hugh de Saint-Cher) is shown concentrating on a manuscript, his spectacles at the end of his nose. Strangely enough, another of Tommaso's forty scholars was the unbespectacled Albertus Maximus, who makes an appearance in the entry for ANDROID.

stall

Here's an oddity: a word that originally meant a standing place has come to designate the most expensive seats in a THEATRE. In the sense of the individual enclosure in a cattle shed where each cow is positioned (or *installed*), *stall* is well over a thousand years old; in the sense of the place you stand in a market, the bench on which you display your wares, it dates back to the fourteenth century. Then in the early nineteenth it was adopted into the theatre. An explanation is given by the journalist George Augustus Sala, who as a youth in the 1840s worked as a scene-painter in the Lyceum Theatre in London. He recorded that, at the Lyceum:

> ... an orchestra has been constructed; that is, a separation of the best part of the pit to the extent of about one-third; each row divided into 'stalls' or single seats at half-a-guinea each.

Presumably the idea was that the *stalls* kept members of the audience separate from each other, whereas in the pit they milled about and encroached on each other's space. That separation was an expensive privilege: half-a-guinea may translate as the meagre-sounding sum of 52½p, but it was a lot of money in the days when a bank clerk might be earning a pound a week.

tabloid

In 1884, the London-based pharmaceutical firm of Burroughs Wellcome registered as a trademark the word *Tabloid* to describe the small, compressed drugs and medicines it produced. It also used the word to describe its tablets of tea – in pre-teabag days, these were made from compressed tea leaves or tea dust, each tablet being enough for one cup. Some nineteen years later Burroughs Wellcome brought a prosecution against a chemist in Manchester that was describing its own products as 'tabloids'. Although the prosecution was successful, the judge remarked that the word had become so widely used that it had acquired the secondary, non-proprietary sense of 'a compressed form or dose of anything'.

Although *tabloid* continued to be used in this sense until well into the twentieth century, it was applied figuratively to other compact products – including newspapers – before that century began. The point about the first tabloid newspapers was not their size; it was that they printed the news itself in condensed, easy-to-read form. The newspaper magnate Lord Northcliffe, who founded both the *Daily Mail* (1896) and the *Daily Mirror* (1903), pioneered a style of writing that was christened *tabloid journalism* as early as 1901. What we now think of as the *tabloid format* – usually 40 x 30 cm – came into being in about 1918 and was widely used by New York scandal sheets in the 1920s, but wasn't adopted by many British nationals (including the *Daily Mail*) until the 1970s.

See also TABLET.

telegenic

The *-genic* part of this word literally means 'productive of' or 'generating' (as in *carcinogenic*, 'causing cancer'). It's loosely related to *gene,* which derives from the Greek for *born.* From this it came to signify 'suitable for', as in *photogenic*, 'suitable for photography' or, more loosely, 'looking good in a photograph'. In this sense *photogenic* was first used in the 1920s and it's a sign of how quickly television became important that *telegenic* – 'looking good on television' – was coined as early as 1939. To put that into perspective, it's little more than a decade after the Scot John Logie Baird and the American Charles Francis Jenkins made the first experimental television broadcasts and only five years after the first cathode-ray televisions were manufactured in Germany.

The first person to be categorized as *telegenic* was the actress Judith Barrett, whom the *Baltimore Sun* described as 'pretty and blonde ... the perfect type of beauty for television ... She is slated for the first television motion picture.' As Ms Barrett retired from films in 1940 and seems never to have appeared on small or large screen again, it would appear either that she found other things to do with her life or that the *Sun* got it wrong.

Looking good is not the only quality connected with television that has spawned a new word. Preachers who use the medium to spread their word have been known as *televangelists* (*television* + *evangelist*) since the 1970s, while a *journalist* who works in *television* has been a *telejournalist* since at least the 1990s. The lengthy televised charity fundraisers known as *telethons* (*television* + *marathon*) have been in existence since as far back as 1949, when the American comedian Milton Berle hosted a programme that raised over a million dollars for cancer research (close to ten million in today's terms) in sixteen hours.

There is also a word *radiogenic*, but – reasonably enough, given the nature of radio – it isn't generally applied to looks. Something described as *radiogenic* is likely to be a play or other broadcast that lends itself well to that medium, relying on sound rather than visuals to achieve its effect.

theatre

The first successful playhouse in London was opened in 1576 and known as The Theatre. It's tempting to write 'known *simply* as The Theatre', but in fact there was nothing simple about it. Plays up until that time had generally been performed in the yards of inns, and to create a formal venue for them was a big step forward. Small wonder, then, that the owner – actor-manager James Burbage (father of Richard, the first person ever to play Hamlet) – should want to give it a grandiose name. Until then, a *theatre* had been what we would now call an amphitheatre, often a vast circular space with tiers of seats rising away from the stage. Burbage's Theatre would have been on a smaller scale – more like Shakespeare's Globe than the Colosseum – but with any luck, he must have thought, the name would pull in the punters.

Part of the point of a theatre was, of course, that the audience should be able to see; that explains the extended use of the word in, for example, *lecture theatre* or *operating theatre*. In the eighteenth century an operating theatre in a hospital was designed like an amphitheatre, so that up to 450 people (some of them paying, as they would for any other entertaining SPECTACLE) could watch what the surgeon was doing.

The figurative sense of 'the place where the action happens', as in *a theatre of war*, emerged almost as soon as the literal one, certainly within Shakespeare's lifetime.

CHAPTER TWO

Sex 'n' Drugs 'n' Rock 'n' Roll

... not to mention food and drink: this chapter looks at words that deal with a whole range of lifestyle choices. A number of them carry the implicit warning, 'Don't try this at home.'

acid

Lysergic acid diethylamide is a hallucinogenic drug whose name is far too long for anyone taking it to bother with. Hence the abbreviations *LSD* and *acid*, closely associated with the hippy movement of the 1960s. It isn't surprising, considering how spaced out most of those involved were, that no one is quite certain how *acid house* or *acid rock* got their names, but a connection with the drug is usually implied. The *house* element seems to be clearer: *house music* was pioneered in the 1980s in a Chicago club called The Warehouse, or The House for short.

See also ROCK.

alcopop

This is a portmanteau of *alcohol* and *pop*, using *pop* in the sense of a non-alcoholic fizzy drink (originally so called because of the popping sound it made when its cork was drawn, although it's a long time since the average soft drink came with a cork). The term *alcopop* has no clear-cut definition and seems to have been coined by journalists in the 1990s to describe an increasingly popular range of sweet, fruity-tasting drinks that contained a surprising amount of alcohol. The production and marketing of *alcopops* quickly became controversial in many countries because of fears that they appealed too strongly to youthful drinkers, but the word remains as a useful description of a wide variety of products.

breathalyser

A way of assessing how much alcohol someone has been drinking by means of having them blow into a bag or plastic tube, a *breath analyser* is a handy device that was first developed in the US, largely by an officer of the Indiana State Police named Robert Borkenstein, who had also done pioneering work on the lie detector. The drink/driving appliance was originally (in the 1930s) known, less subtly, as a *drunkometer*. Borkenstein registered *Breathalyzer* as a trademark in the late 1950s, but the word has passed into general use, without the initial capital.

The verb *to breathalyse* is what is called a back-formation, meaning in this case that it developed from the noun rather than the other way around, but it was in use by 1967. That was the year in which the UK first introduced a legal limit to the amount of alcohol drivers should have in their bloodstream:

clearly once the breathalyser was in use, police and journalists alike needed a verb to describe what you did with it.

brunch

In 1895 the British writer Guy Beringer wrote a piece in *Hunter's Weekly* entitled 'Brunch: A Plea'. Recognizing that those who had been out on the town on a Saturday night might not want to get up early enough on Sunday to have *breakfast* before church, nor to face the heavy roast *lunch* that would normally be served shortly afterwards, he advocated a meal that was a combination of the two. *Brunch*, he explained, was 'cheerful, sociable and inciting ... It puts you in a good temper, it makes you satisfied with yourself and your fellow beings, it sweeps away the worries and cobwebs of the week.' A surprising number of people must have read *Hunter's Weekly*: within a year *Punch* was suggesting that 'to be fashionable nowadays we must "brunch"'.

Despite its British origins, brunch became popular in the US in the 1930s and soon came to incorporate dishes such as eggs Benedict, which used traditional breakfast ingredients in a non-traditional way, and at the same time helped soak up any alcohol left over from the night before. The fact that brunch was aimed at those who may not have been at their best also explains why it was often accompanied by a Bloody Mary, widely regarded as an effective hangover cure.

That early *Punch* article gave a further detail that seems never to have caught on, however: if the meal was eaten only a little after breakfast time, the magazine explained, it was called *brunch*; much later, so that it became an early lunch, it was *blunch*. This was surely too fine a distinction to appeal to those who were feeling a bit bleary-eyed after a late night.

As a footnote to the above, a TWEET from the QI Elves reports that in 1896 the manufacturers of Shredded Wheat recommended serving their recently launched cereal with melted cheese, oysters or poached eggs on top. Given the date, you have to assume that they were jumping – perhaps misguidedly – on the new brunch bandwagon.

chaperone

Chaperon (without the final *e*) is a French word for a hood and was used as such in English from the fourteenth century. In the eighteenth, when young ladies were not permitted to go out without an older or married woman to keep an eye on them, the word was adopted – sometimes with the *e* on the end, which non-French-speaking English folk apparently thought made it look feminine – to denote that companion. An 1864 entry in *Notes and Queries* gives the rather sweet explanation that 'the experienced married woman shelters the youthful *débutante* as a hood shelters the face'.

cougar

The mountain lion, puma or cougar (*Puma concolor*) is the largest wild cat in North America: there are perhaps 30,000 of them in the United States alone, mostly in and west of the Rockies, although they are found as far north as Canada and as far south as Argentina. (By way of comparison, there are probably 15,000 wild jaguars – the other American big cat – in the entire world, and their range extends only from Mexico to Argentina.) The word *cougar* entered English from French in the eighteenth century, but was an adaptation of the indigenous South American name.

According to the website of Defenders of Wildlife, cougars are solitary animals, actively avoiding other cats except during courtship but travelling long distances in search of food. 'They hunt alone and attack from behind, breaking the neck of their prey by biting it at the base of the skull. After killing their prey, they will bury it and leave it, coming back to feed on it when hungry.'

Defenders of Wildlife say nothing about the females actively seeking the companionship of younger males. Absolutely nothing. Information on that bizarre variation in meaning comes from a piece published in the *Star* Online in 2007, written by lexicographer Grant Barrett. He traces the first use of *cougar* meaning a woman who has sex with younger men to a website called cougardate.com; it was, Barrett says, given its name by the nephew of one of the founders, who compared the women in question to 'cougars in search of small defenceless animals'. The *Star* article gives the term a 'first recorded use' date of 1999, which puts it two years ahead of 'relationship expert' Valerie Gibson's book *Cougar: A guide for older women dating younger men*. There's no doubt, though, that this book and the later TV sitcom *Cougar Town* helped to popularize the term.

crack

This is one that you *really* shouldn't try at home. If you mix cocaine with baking powder (of all unlikely substances) and water, heat it until it hardens, then break it into small pieces, the result is *crack*, apparently because of the crackling noise it makes when you heat it. The name has been around since the 1980s, as have associated expressions such as *crack house* and *crack head*. It's not to be confused with CRUNCH, which (when applied to credit) gets you into difficulties for entirely different reasons.

gay

Someone described as *gay* in the fourteenth century was cheerful and carefree; by the seventeenth they were likely to be a bit feckless and self-indulgent – it was then that the word took on a disapproving edge. It could even, when applied to a woman, mean she was a prostitute. In the early twentieth century it began to be used to describe homosexuals – mostly by the homosexuals themselves, as a sort of insiders' slang. It wasn't until Gay Liberation became a political and social issue in the 1960s that the word 'came out' into the mainstream and gradually developed into a widely used, non-pejorative term for a homosexual of either gender.

Then, sometime in the 1970s, it regained that offensive edge and by the early years of the twenty-first century was recorded as being the most frequently used term of abuse among schoolchildren. Although concerns are often expressed about the implied homophobia, most children use it in a way that has nothing to do with sex – it's simply an alternative for 'lame', 'feeble' or 'pathetically unaware of fashion'. Even so, it's unpleasant and may mean we have to come up with another acceptable colloquialism for homosexuality soon.

Those who claim to be good at detecting that another person is gay boast of the efficiency of their *gaydar* (*gay* + *radar*). This term appears to have emerged in the 1980s, but – given the obsessiveness with which some people treat the subject – one contributor to an online FORUM may not have been far wrong when he suggested that it had been around 'since about a week after radar was invented'.

gig

In the sense of what might more formally be called a concert engagement, a *gig* is listed as 'of unknown origin' in the dictionaries. This doesn't stop people speculating, though. There are those who say it is short for *engagement*; others who connect it with *gigue*, a French word for a lively dance that derives from the English *jig*. Still others drag in a different meaning of *gig* – a light, open, one-horse carriage – and say that black musicians in New Orleans used to perform on such a carriage so that they wouldn't be arrested for playing in the street. This seems unlikely to me, as even where segregation was at its most entrenched, black musicians seem to have been allowed to play in marching bands as well as in brothels and black bars.

Whatever the truth, the word – originally referring to a musical one-night stand – was used in the magazine *Melody Maker* in 1926 and was well established by the end of the 1930s.

joint

The basic definition of a *joint* is 'the place at which two parts are joined together' – thus the *hip joint* which joins the torso to the leg or the *dovetail joint* whereby two parts of a piece of furniture are neatly interlocked. In twentieth-century drug-related slang, a *joint* originally included all the kit that a user required – the syringe and needles for an injector, the pipe for the opium smoker, not to mention the actual drug. When, in the 1960s, smoking marijuana became the common form of 'recreational' drug-taking, the name transferred to the cigarette itself.

metrosexual

A combination of *metropolitan* and *sexual*, this was coined in the 1990s to describe a growing breed of city-dwelling men who were overtly concerned with grooming and personal appearance. The subtext was that, although such men were usually heterosexual, their habits and interests resembled those stereotypically attributed to homosexuals. But there is nothing sexual implied in this word. When a television comedian said, 'I thought it meant men who got up to dodgy things on the underground,' it was safe to assume that he was joking.

Muzak

This is a proprietary name – hence the capital letter and the ® sign that is usually found with it – but it has become widely used without either of those embellishments and is also sometimes spelled *musak*. Strictly speaking, *Muzak* is a system that enables recorded music to be played through speakers in shops and other public places; it was patented in the US by Muzak LLC in 1935. However, *muzak* quickly came to refer to the sort of music usually played *through* the system – bland, middle-of-the-road tunes designed to provide a gentle background rather than be listened to, the sort of stuff now often dismissed as *elevator music*.

However, muzak once had a much higher purpose: in 1978 the wonderfully named Bing Muscio, then president of the Muzak Company, told the *Palm Beach Daily News* that one of its aims was to improve productivity in the workplace. In theory at least, playing such music reduced the impact of downswings that many workers felt at regular and predictable intervals through the day: after an hour and a half at work, again half an hour before lunch and then again in the middle of the afternoon. 'Muzak' was also specifically chosen to combat the Monday blues and the boredom of Fridays.

Four years before this interview, Bing had told *The New York Times* the origin of the BRAND: 'We needed a catchy name and the best known trade name at that time was Kodak. So we just combined Kodak and music and got Muzak.'

pot

Drug slang tends to be a law unto itself and no one is quite sure why *pot* came to mean cannabis, as it did in the 1930s. Links to the Mexican Spanish *potaguaya* or *potiguaya*, a corruption of *potación de guaya* or 'drink of grief' (a concoction of marijuana leaves soaked in something alcoholic) have been suggested but not corroborated. The fact that you can grow it in a *flower pot* on your windowsill is certainly a coincidence.

punk

There aren't many words that in the course of their history have drifted back and forth between the genders, but this is one of them. When, in the famous scene from *Dirty Harry*, Clint Eastwood, carrying a .44 Magnum that may or may not have a bullet left in it, wonders about feeling lucky, he addresses his potential victim – a young man – as 'punk'. He means a worthless petty criminal, one the world wouldn't miss much if Harry did, as threatened, 'blow his head clean off'. That film was made in 1971 and Harry's meaning had been current for some time in gangster-style dialogue – Dashiell Hammett's 'hard-boiled' detective Sam Spade had used it in *The Maltese Falcon*, published way back in 1929.

Also in 1971, the term *punk rock* (attributed to the American music critic Dave Marsh, famous for his acerbic comments on the musicians he reviewed) was first applied to a certain sort of music, distinguished by its anti-Establishment lyrics and weird spiky haircuts.

But the word is a lot older than the *punk movement* or *Dirty Harry* and used to apply exclusively to females. In Shakespeare's time it meant a prostitute. In *Measure for Measure* (c. 1603), the Duke is questioning Mariana, who claims not to be married, nor to be a maid (meaning an unmarried girl, assumed to be a virgin) or a widow. 'You are nothing then?' he queries. 'Neither maid, widow, nor wife?' One of his attendants interposes helpfully, 'My lord, she may be a punk; for many of them are neither maid, widow, nor wife.' (In fact, Mariana means that she is a jilted fiancée, but we needn't worry about that here.) The sense of being not necessarily a prostitute but certainly 'a woman of easy virtue' persisted into the twentieth century, as did the parallel sense of a male prostitute or a man forced into a homosexual relationship, especially in prison. Nowadays, however, these senses are used only in a historical context or in prison slang; most people would understand *punk* to refer to the music, its performers and its fans – of either sex.

rock

Rocking and *rolling* were originally two separate actions: in the seventeenth century they meant the pitching and tossing of a ship – you *rocked* one way then, with a bit of luck, *rolled* back the other. By that time *rocking* had already been in use for many centuries to describe the gentler movement used to lull a baby to sleep. But the idea and the alliteration of *rocking and rolling* appealed to the lyricist Sidney Clare, who in 1934 provided the words for a song called 'Rock and Roll', featured on the soundtrack of the film *Transatlantic Merry-Go-Round*. The action of the movie takes place aboard an ocean liner and Clare's lyrics were the first to link the action of a ship to the movement of a dance: his singers tell us that they are 'in the spell of the rollin', rockin' rhythm of the sea'.

A few years later, another American songwriter, Buck Ram, came up with a new song called 'Rock and Roll', this time dispensing with the ship. He encouraged his characters to 'rock and roll' while the band was playing and, while they were at it, to 'keep their shoulders swaying'.

More recent lyricists in search of a rhyme must be grateful to Buck Ram: bodies have been swayin' while music has been playin' in many, many popular songs ever since. From this rhythmic dance movement evolved the concept of *rock and roll* (or, soon, *rock 'n' roll*) music; this in turn was shortened – by 1956, the year in which Elvis Presley had his first hits – to *rock*. Any subsequent form of rock music – whether ACID or *glam* or *prog* – owes part of its name to the people who first likened dancing to being on board a ship.

toast

Why, you may wonder, should we have the same word for grilled bread and for drinking to someone's health? The answer is that the grilled bread was frequently dunked in wine or some other beverage: Shakespeare's Sir John Falstaff, in *The Merry Wives of Windsor*, orders one of his servants to 'fetch me a quart of sack; put a toast in't' – a token gesture towards soaking up all the wine he gets through in the course of the play. A hundred years after Shakespeare, some bright spark thought of likening a lady whose health one drank to the piece of toast that livened up the drink. As the journalist Richard Steele explained in an early edition of *Tatler*, it was 'a new Name found out by the Wits to make a Lady have the same Effect as Burridge in the Glass when a Man is drinking'. (*Burridge* is *borage*, a herb often added to drinks such as punch to give a bit of zest.) Thus the lady herself became *the toast* – often *the toast of the season* or *a reigning toast*, the one it was fashionable for all the young bachelors to be in love with.

The idea that the toast was the *act* of drinking the health of someone or something, such as one's regiment or one's country, had appeared by the mid-eighteenth century, as had the concept of a *toastmaster*, one who at a formal banquet was in charge of proposing the toasts. *Toastmistress* isn't recorded until the 1920s, presumably because the idea of a female taking on this role would have been anathema (to the men) in earlier times.

CHAPTER THREE

Hi- and Lo-Tech

You'd think that all of the developments in computers and IT over the last half-century or so would require a whole range of new vocabulary. And indeed they do – this is by far the longest chapter in the book. What's perhaps surprising is how much of that vocabulary has been with us for centuries, in one guise or another.

android

The late 1970s were a boom period for *androids*, partly thanks to the 1979 film *Alien* (whose sequels, of course, introduced them to a younger generation). But to lovers of *A Hitchhiker's Guide to the Galaxy* – which first hit our radios way back in 1978, before appearing as books, television series and films – the word will always conjure up the whining robot Marvin, the 'paranoid android' ('Life? Don't talk to me about life'). Although the whining is optional, an *android* was originally a human-shaped robot, with the word deriving from the Greek for 'in the form of a man'.

That meaning of *robot* wasn't used in English until the 1920s, but the first recorded use of *android* is as early as 1728. Ephraim Chambers' *Cyclopaedia* of that year defines it as 'an Automaton, in figure of a Man; which by virtue of certain Springs, etc. duly contrived, Walks, Speaks, etc.' It then adds the intriguing information that 'Albertus Magnus is recorded as having made an Androides'. Albertus Magnus is now a Roman Catholic saint, but in his lifetime he caused a certain amount of upset: against the wishes of his church he studied Aristotle and other classical authors and, according to an early twentieth-century source, 'owing to his profound knowledge he did not escape the imputation of using magical arts and trafficking with the Evil One'. He sounds like just the sort of man who might have created an early replica human – which, given that he died in 1280, would have put him well ahead of his time.

As for the modern sense of *android*, it is simply the name of the company that produces the massively successful MOBILE-phone operating system and continues to develop variations far too quickly to be recorded here. None of them, so far as I know, is yet in human shape ...

battery

This is related to the French *battre*, to beat, and the earliest meanings are connected with beating or *battering*. By the sixteenth century, a *battery* came to be 'the apparatus used in beating or battering', specifically pieces of artillery; it was also a small unit of artillerymen.

From the idea that little pieces of artillery could be put together to produce quite an onslaught came the thought that a number of simple instruments could be combined to make a more sophisticated one. This turned out to be particularly useful in the field of electricity: by 1748 the American polymath Benjamin Franklin was writing about 'what we call'd *an electrical-battery*, consisting of eleven panes of large sash-glass, arm'd with thin leaden plates' and linked by wire and CHAIN 'so that the whole might be charged together, and with the same labour as one single pane'. Batteries today are somewhat smaller than eleven sash windows, but the idea of linking positive and negative CELLS in the same device persists in those little things you put in torches and CAMERAS to make them work.

The word has also come to have broader uses, as when a doctor doesn't know what's wrong with you and submits you to *a battery of tests*, or someone with scant concern for animal welfare puts a whole lot of cages together and rears *battery chickens*.

bit

Most portmanteau words – see, for example, ADVERTORIAL and BREATHALYSER – are a reasonable length; they are, after all, made up of parts of two words put together. So *bit* – short for *binary digit* – must be the shortest example of its kind on record. The *binary digits* are 0 and 1, the only two digits used in *binary notation*. A single binary digit (either 0 or 1) represents the smallest unit of information in computing – so it's quite appropriate that it should be designated by one of the smallest words.

Coinage of the term is attributed to the American mathematician John Wilder Tukey in about 1948. He's said to have revolutionized the way statisticians think and however little you may understand about statistics you have to applaud Tukey for realizing that *binit* wouldn't have been an ideal abbreviation.

Bitmap has been in use since the early 1970s. It is, obviously, a combination of *bit* and *map* and means a method of organizing a graphic display in which one or more bits of information are assigned to each PIXEL.

blog

Short for WEB + *log*, this uses *log* in the sense of a journal (you remember: 'Captain's log, star date 41153.7'). The concept of a personal diary or expressions of opinion being written online dates to the 1990s, with the abbreviation recorded almost immediately. An excellent description, cited by the OED from the *Salina (Kansas) Journal* in 2002 – when there were still lots of people out there who didn't know what *blogs* were – explains that they 'contain daily musings about news, dating, marriage, divorce, children, politics in the Middle East ... or millions of other things or nothing at all'.

The 'journal' meaning of *log* comes from a time when a ship's progress was literally reckoned by a piece of wood the vessel dragged along in its wake; hence a *log book* was something in which you entered the readings taken from the *log*. So from the nineteenth century *to log*, in addition to meaning 'to cut down trees', came to mean 'to enter in a log book, to keep a record of'. (A vessel or vehicle could also *log up* a certain number of miles/kilometres, meaning that there would be a record of its having travelled that distance.) *Logging in/out/on/off* on a computer dates from the 1960s and comes from this sense of keeping a record: the computer registers the time the action takes place and, because the user generally has to enter a password, knows who that user is. There's nowhere to hide.

An inevitable development of the *web log* was the *video blog* or *vlog*, pioneered in the early years of this century. It really took off with the growth of YouTube from about 2007 and has made celebrities of, among others, Zoe Sugg (Zoella), Alfie Deyes and Shay Carl. Carl is working on what is probably the world's first *vlogumentary* and there are sure to be other new words emerging from these sources any day now.

bug

The oldest meaning for this word (which survives in *bugbear*) is an object of fear, often an imaginary one. From this, in the seventeenth century, came the generalized name for an insect that is still widely used in American English. From this in turn came the idea of a *bug* as a problem in a machine or system: the *Pall Mall Gazette* of 1889 refers to the inventor Thomas Edison 'discovering "a bug" in his phonograph – an expression for solving a difficulty, and implying that some imaginary insect has secreted itself inside and is causing all the trouble'.

That appealing piece of imagery was picked up by other people and was well established in technical jargon by the time of the Second World War. Then, in 1945, naval officer Grace Hopper found a moth stuck in the works of the pioneering computer Harvard Mark II. She went to the trouble of sticking the moth into her LOG book with the annotation 'first actual case of bug being found'. It's not often that the imaginative use of a word comes along half a century before the literal one.

As a mini-digression here, it's worth observing that for the first 250 years of its existence, *computer* referred to a person, one whose job it was to *compute*, to do calculations of greater or lesser complexity.

bulb

The defining factor of a *bulb* is its shape – rounded and swollen, like a balloon that has been fully blown up. The word comes from the Greek for onion and if you'd gone to the market in the sixteenth century to buy a bulb, an onion is what you'd have come home with. What gardeners now call bulbs – the compressed stems which are planted underground and from which tulips, daffodils and other flowers grow – are so named because they are onion-shaped. This sense came into being in the seventeenth century, shortly after tulips had been introduced to western Europe and bulbs, changing hands for vast sums of money, were a hot topic of conversation.

It is from the shape that more scientific senses come, too. The physicist Daniel Fahrenheit used the Dutch word for bulb to describe the swollen bit of glass at the end of the mercury-in-glass thermometer he invented in 1714; and, after many other scientists had worked on the idea, Thomas Edison patented the *electric light bulb* in 1880. Put a standard light bulb alongside a bulb from the garden centre, screw your eyes up just a little and you'll see the resemblance.

camera

Camera is the Latin for a room, particularly a private one, so that when a judge hears a court case *in camera* it is in the absence of the public and the media. The *camera obscura* or 'dark chamber' is a precursor of the modern photographic camera, based on the observation (made by Aristotle in the fourth century BC, but possibly older than that) that light passing through a small hole into a darkened room produces an image on a wall opposite. It was used for centuries in various parts of the world by scientists studying the movement of light, by astronomers observing the sun and by artists learning about perspective. Although originally referring to a room, the expression *camera obscura* was also, by the nineteenth century, applied to something no larger than a box that worked on the same principle, projecting images on to a wall or large screen – for entertainment as well as for scientific purposes.

As the concept of photography developed, the fact that the word *camera* had derived from the room rather than the device was pushed aside, and it came to be applied to the little box that used an aperture and a lens to shed light and therefore an image on the film within. That use is recorded in 1840, when modern photography was in its infancy; when 'movies' came into being half a century later it was easy to apply the same term to the apparatus that produced their images too.

cell

Back in the mists of time, a *cell* was a dwelling made up of a single room, or the room itself – often very small. From there it became the confined space occupied by a monk or nun, or by a prisoner. Then it acquired various more or less scientific meanings: it was a synonym for 'pore', or one of the units that made up a honeycomb, or the basic unit of a battery. It wasn't until well into the nineteenth century that it attained its most common modern meaning, that of the basic unit of living matter, which produces energy, synthesizes more complex substances from raw materials, and can usually either divide or replicate itself. Some cells measure as little as a hundredth of a millimetre across, so it's not surprising that scientists took a while to identify and name them.

The underlying meaning that unites all these senses is that of the building block, the simple single unit that can be combined with others to make something more complicated. From this, in the latter part of the twentieth century, came *cellular radio* – a system that divides an area into *cells*, each of which contains a fixed-location transmitter and whose receiving equipment automatically picks up the signal from the nearest transmitter when the receiver moves from one cell to another. These cells are often hexagonal, allowing them to fit neatly together and tying in happily with the honeycomb connection mentioned above. The MOBILE telephone uses this technology and for that reason is given (in North America and other parts of the English-speaking world) the alternative name of *cellular telephone*, *cellphone* or simply *cell*.

So from being something that kept a convict in one place, isolated from his fellow human beings, a cell has become a device that encourages everyone to move around as much as they choose and still stay in touch.

cookie

Why the word for a small, crisp-baked cake (what the British call a biscuit) should have come to be used for the package of data that enables a PROGRAM to remember a specific user is one of the minor mysteries of modern life. It seems to have been first used with reference to Nexis computers in the 1980s, and in those early days the expression was sometimes a *magic cookie*, sometimes just a *cookie*. But why? Nobody knows.

That said, a website called The Cookie Controller not only offers four possible explanations, it asks readers to vote for their favourite. My favourite, for what it is worth, is the Cookie Monster theory. This suggests that an unnamed programmer left an unnamed corporation for unspecified reasons, and after his departure the company found that its system would randomly and all too frequently crash. It would display the message 'Gimme a cookie' and refuse to work until the word 'cookie' was entered into the system. Nothing the IT department could do would solve this glitch, so they worked round it by teaching users how to 'give the machine a cookie' whenever it asked for one.

Given that the TV series *Sesame Street* and *The Muppets* were at the height of their popularity at the time, and that the Cookie Monster, with his constant demands for cookies, was a much-loved and much-quoted character, this explanation surely has a ring of truth. Setting a system to cause mindless disruption in the style of a Muppet strikes me as just the sort of thing a disgruntled programmer might do. In any case, there seems to be nothing in the dictionaries to refute the story.

digital

Back in the fifteenth century *digital* was a noun as well as an adjective and meant the same as *digit*: a single-figure number. Like *digit*, *digital* could also be used to mean a finger – a single element in a set of ten – and a *digital number* was anything from nought to nine. When computers came along they started to record information in binary form (see BIT), which meant using the digits zero and one. Thus *digital* came to be used for appliances that recorded information in this way, such as a *digital camera*, which made it unnecessary to use film; and also for those that used figures to *display* information. A *digital clock* shows the time as, for example, 2:10, whereas the traditional clock face with its moving hands indicates this as ten past two.

These old-fashioned clock faces and other non-digital ways of transmitting information are described as *analogue*. From the Greek meaning 'proportional', this term has been around since the early nineteenth century and can mean, for example, parts of an animal or plant that have evolved in different ways but ended up with similar functions. Come the 1940s, the word was adopted into early techno-speak to describe mechanisms that use something variable – a moving part (such as the hands of a clock) or a changing frequency (in AM or

FM radio) – to do their measuring. This variety is what makes *analogue* different from *digital*, which relies on the simple on/off system of binary.

disc

A *disc*, or in computer language usually a *disk*, is a flat circular plate. The word comes from the Ancient Greek for 'to throw' and the connection can be traced via the *discus*, which has been thrown in the Olympics since classical times and was and is shaped like a – well, like a flat circular plate. Or a disc. Since then, we have used the word to describe a range of similarly shaped things, from the flat bones between the vertebrae in the spine to the circles of shellac and then vinyl that formed gramophone records. Latterly – since the mid-twentieth century – we have had hard disks and FLOPPY disks and compact discs and DIGITAL video (or versatile) discs to store and read information. They're all flat and round, is the point.

domain

To the uninitiated, an internet PROTOCOL (IP) address is no more than a random set of figures separated by dots. To those in the know, however, it is the unique identifying number given to any device connected to the internet. It's like a cross between a telephone number (which allows other machines to contact yours) and a car registration number (which proves that you own something and gives a hint as to your location).

What the uninitiated recognize and make sense of is the *domain name*, the distinctive name of a network that is used as part of an internet address: microsoft. com, for example, or pinterest.com. A *domain* may consist of any number of linked computers (all with different IP addresses) that come together to provide a service or a certain type of information.

This use came into being with the internet in the 1980s, but the word had been around for several hundred years before that. Its origins can be traced back to the Latin *dominus*, meaning 'master'; in earlier times, and still sometimes used this way, a *domain* was the land over which one had *dominion* or mastery. It also has the figurative meaning of 'a field of knowledge, an area of expertise', but nowadays a *domain* is most commonly the specific part of the internet over which one person or company exercises control.

drive

The verb *to drive* is much older than the noun: we have been *driving* our oxen or *driving* other people away for a thousand years. Early meanings of the noun kept that sense of impetus: in the seventeenth century the expression *full drive* meant what we would now mean by *at full tilt* – moving fast and furiously.

Then gradually a drive became a more gentle thing, in the sense of *going for a drive* – not heading for anywhere in particular, just taking the air, originally in a horse-drawn vehicle and, by the late nineteenth century, in that newfangled invention, the motor car. It was also a place where you could go for that drive: the *carriage-drive*, *carriage-way* or *drive-way*, as opposed to the *foot-path*, where you were supposed to walk. *Driveway* soon dispensed with the hyphen and became specifically the paved path leading from a public road along which you drove your car in order to reach your house and put the vehicle in the garage.

But the sense of impelling or pressurizing never entirely went away: a *drive* in tennis or golf is a powerful shot; and a person who has *drive* is energetic and ambitious and may be described as a *driving force*. So, with the spread of mechanization, came the idea of a *drive* as something that made something else work: a motorbike engine might have a *belt drive*, for instance, while a bicycle had a *drive chain.* All of which meant that when, in the middle of the twentieth century, early computers needed something to *drive* their *disks*, the word was up and running, just waiting to be adopted.

See also DISC.

drone

There are pros and cons to being a drone. If you're a bee, that is. Drones do no work, don't have to look after the hive and don't have to go out and forage for pollen. All they do is eat the honey the worker bees provide, build up their strength, then go and look for a queen bee and mate with her.

So far so good, you might think. The down side is that the sexual act kills them.

This sense of *drone* has been around for a thousand years and more, but then people have been keeping and studying bees for a long time (Pliny the Elder, who died when Vesuvius erupted in AD 79, was very keen on them and devoted a sizeable chunk of his *Natural History* to them. He noted that drones didn't have a sting and thought that they were an 'imperfect' bee, 'doomed ... to be the slaves of the genuine bees'). The figurative use, meaning someone who lives off the labours of others, appears in the sixteenth century, and it's probably this meaning that encouraged the inventors of the UAV or Unmanned Aerial Vehicle, during and immediately after the Second World War, to give their brainchild this nickname. The earliest UAVs, after all, were operated remotely: somebody back at Mission Control was doing the work. More recent technology enables them to be pre-programmed to follow a certain course and conduct reconnaissance, drop a bomb, deliver a parcel or just fool around in the park, so the drone imagery is even stronger: once the programming is done, it could be argued, *no one* is doing the work.

Speaking of recent technology, a frightening glimpse of the future shows that, with the SELFIE stick having been banned in many public places, eager self-photographers are taking to carrying around their own private drones so that they can snap themselves standing next to the *Mona Lisa* from further away than arm's length. That buzzing sound you hear next time you are in the Louvre may not be an extra-large fly ...

emoticon

This is an ICON expressing *emotion*, like the smiley face people put in texts to indicate 'I'm only joking' or 'I've received your news and I'm pleased about it'. NETIQUETTE advises against the overuse of these devices, but, as the *St Louis (Missouri) Post-Dispatch* put it in 1994, 'The lack of intonation and other cues used to convey irony, sarcasm and self-deprecation in speech can lead to misunderstandings on the screen. (This is where a well-placed smiley-face or two comes in handy.)'

The word *emoticon* dates only from the 1980s, but the concept has been around for rather longer. In 1912, the satirical writer Ambrose Bierce proposed 'an improvement in punctuation – the snigger point, or note of cachinnation', which looked like a smiling mouth and was to be added to 'every jocular or ironical sentence'. He probably thought he was joking.

Hard on the heels of the emoticon comes the Japanese-born *emoji*, also a DIGITAL icon used to express emotion, but more sophisticated in terms of imagery than those that are created by pressing a colon followed by a parenthesis. *Emoji* is made up of the Japanese for *picture* (*e*) and *character* (*moji*), so its resemblance to *emotion* and *emoticon* is a particularly happy coincidence.

file

The Latin *filum* means a line or thread, so that in English the earliest meanings of *file* include the figurative *thread of life* or *thread of an argument*. In the sixteenth century a *file* was also a thread or wire on which papers – bills, archives, that sort of thing – were hung so that they could be kept in order and easily referred to. From this the word came to apply to other ways in which documents could be stored, notably a *folder* containing all the papers pertaining to a certain subject or court case; and by extension the contents of such a file, such as an employee's *personnel file*. A folder, of course, was a folded piece of cardboard, leather or other casing, which enclosed the papers.

Come the computer age, then, *file* was a handy word to adopt for a collection of related records or data. It has been used in this sense since the mid-twentieth century. And, in computing, as in a court room or old-fashioned office, files that need to be kept together are stored in a *folder* – even though there is no longer any folding involved.

flash

This is a word with a vast number of related meanings, but the main thing they have in common is that they last only a matter of seconds. From *a flash in the pan* or a *newsflash* to *flash-frying* a piece of steak, almost anything that's done *in a flash* is over very quickly. Lots of flashes are also to do with bursts of light: either *a flash of lightning* or the sort of on-off *flashing* light that you might see in a lighthouse or on top of a police car.

From a combination of these two meanings came the *flashbulb* and *flashgun* – both now generally just called a *flash* – used in photography to produce a quick burst of brightness and enable the photographer to capture an image in poor light conditions. *Flash photography* was developed by the 1890s, originally by burning magnesium (which produces a particularly bright flame), later through the magic of electricity.

What Americans call a *flashlight* is something of a misnomer as, provided the BATTERY is charged, it will provide a continuous beam of light. Brits call this a *torch*, which is a name that covers all sorts of portable lights, some of them flaming.

Then there is the computing *flash drive,* so called because it uses *flash memory.* This in turn is so called because it can be read or written to more quickly than other, less sophisticated forms of memory. At the speed of lightning, perhaps.

floppy

Floppy DISKS are now more or less obsolete, having given way to USB FLASH drives, email attachments and the Cloud, but there was a time – and not so very long ago – when they seemed a revelation. The idea that you could shove a disk measuring 5¼ inches (just over 13 cm) in diameter into a computer, transfer information onto it and carry it from place to place without the use of paper was a real eye-opener in the 1970s. The fact that a floppy could hold perhaps 1.2 MB of information – a risibly small quantity by today's standards – didn't make it any the less impressive.

The original floppy disks were indeed a bit floppy – an adjective that had been around since the mid-nineteenth century – though in the 1980s Amstrad and others produced a range of computers that took 3-inch or 3½-inch (about 7.5 cm or 9 cm) disks with a hard outer coating that meant they *didn't* flop. Nonetheless, the name had become established and it persisted. What seems strange now is that a *hard copy* means something that is printed on paper, surely the floppiest medium of them all.

focus

The Latin *focus* means 'hearth' or 'fireplace', and perhaps because the hearth was the symbolic centre of a household, in the seventeenth century *focus* was adopted into English in various scientific contexts to mean another sort of symbolic centre: a point where lines, waves or particles converged or from which they originated. It's this sense that applies to *focus* in photography – it is defined as 'the position in which an object must be situated so that the image produced is clearly defined' and to be *in focus* is to be sharply delineated.

During and after the Second World War, all sorts of people from government ministers to marketing executives began to make use of the *focus group*, a group of people gathered together to *focus on* and discuss a particular issue. Their opinions enabled researchers to assess the effectiveness of anything from wartime propaganda to the packaging of a new product. The concept became popular in the post-war period largely thanks to the work of American sociologist Robert K. Merton at the Bureau of Applied Social Research at Columbia University; the term was coined around the same time by Ernest Dichter, the Austrian-born but by then New York-based father of 'motivational research'.

format

Many terms used to describe how you edit a document on a computer come from old-fashioned printing. *Cut and paste* is one; *format* is another. The format of a book is its size and shape, given either in millimetres or inches, or denoted by names such as *royal*, *crown*, *quarto* and *octavo*, which indicate either the size of the original sheet of paper or the number of times it has been folded. The sense of the word *format* was extended in the twentieth century to include other aspects of presentation, such as the size of a photograph or the way a radio or television show was put together: considerations such as whether or not it had a presenter, or contained interviews with members of the public, or included singing and dancing might all contribute to a show's *format*.

In computing terms, *format* was an easy word to adopt when it came to describing the arrangement of data in a FILE or instruction. It's typical of the late-twentieth-century view that 'any noun can be verbed' that, within a decade or so of *format* being taken into the IT world in the 1950s, someone realized how useful *to format* would be. The noun had existed for well over a century, but no one seems to have thought of using it as a verb in any of its earlier senses.

forum

In the Ancient Roman Empire, a *forum* was a marketplace and The Forum the principal market-place in Rome itself. Like marketplaces across the world and throughout history, it was a place for people to gather and exchange news as well as goods. The Roman Forum was also the focus of political life – you can still see the ruins of the Senate House and the Rostra from which speeches were made. Thus a *forum* came to be any place – literal or figurative – where discussions, particularly on a specific subject, could be held. Towards the end of the twentieth century, when such discussions began to be held online, it seemed logical to call them what they had always been called in the non-VIRTUAL world.

graphic

Graphein was the Ancient Greek for *to draw* or *to write*, and all sorts of words such as *photography* (literally 'drawing with light') and *geography* ('writing about the earth') come from it. *Graphite*, the grey-black stuff inside a pencil, has the same root and *graphic* originally meant to do with writing or drawing. From this we developed *the graphic arts*, *graphic designers* and, as early as the seventeenth century, the idea that a *graphic description* was particularly lifelike: it 'drew a picture' with words.

It wasn't until the nineteenth century that the adjective became a noun, so that we could have *graphics* to illustrate a problem in geometry and, a hundred years later, *computer graphics*, which produced diagrams and the like without the aid of a pencil. In the meantime the adjective had developed two new senses. From having been a compliment, describing something as *graphic* had come to suggest that it contained a fair smattering of sex and violence; and a lengthy form of comic book was being called a *graphic novel.* Even though it was in comic-book form, a graphic novel could tackle serious subjects: Art Spiegelman's *Maus* deals with surviving the Holocaust and is the only example of the genre to date to have won the prestigious Pulitzer Prize.

hack

The OED online delightfully defines *hacking* as 'the use of a computer for the satisfaction it gives' and quotes *The Sunday Times* of 9 December 1984: 'Hacking is totally intellectual – nothing goes boom and there are no sparks. It's your mind against the computer.' That may well be, but when you follow its cross-reference to *hacker* you find the words 'gain unauthorized access', and that's what the word has come to mean to most people. It comes from *hack* in the sense of 'to chop fiercely but randomly' – presumably the implication is that computer hackers can cut into anything they fancy (making a random choice) and leave whatever they have hacked in a mess.

hardware

An eighteenth-century example given in the OED mentions 'locks, hinges, cast-iron and other branches of hardware', and for several hundred years this was what *hardware* meant – all sorts of ironmongery and metal bits and pieces for the home. It still has this sense in the ever-decreasing number of independent *hardware stores*, although most modern hardware stores will also sell you paint and paintbrushes, light BULBS and brooms. From the nineteenth century onwards, *hardware* has been used to refer to other metal objects: weapons, specifically guns, but also jewellery, medals and, since the 1940s, the physical components of a computing system.

Hardware's now widely used counterpart *software*, meaning the PROGRAMS and systems required to make the hardware do something useful, wasn't invented until 1960: it was never used to describe the paint, light bulbs and so forth mentioned in the previous paragraph.

Freeware – free software, available for anyone to use without payment – and *shareware – software* that is *shared* freely for a limited period or with limited features, beyond which it must be paid for – both came into being around the 1980s.

hashtag

Hash is the # sign, used to precede a number or to designate a function key on a telephone keypad. Although it has various other names, strictly speaking it is called an *octothorp*, for reasons that are not entirely clear: the OED cites one Don Macpherson, an employee of Bell Laboratories in the 1960s, who apparently decreed that as the symbol had eight points it should employ the prefix *octo-*; he was also part of a campaign to get Jim Thorpe's medals back from Sweden, so he added *thorp* (not *thorpe*) as a unique element to his word.

If that means nothing to you, you need to know that Jim Thorpe was an American athlete who did fabulously well at the 1912 Olympics in Stockholm, but was then disgraced and stripped of his titles on the grounds that he had violated his amateur status by playing professional baseball three years earlier. After a massive campaign on his behalf, Thorpe was finally reinstated to his former glory in 1982, a mere twenty-nine years after his death.

The reasons an octothorp is called a *hash sign* are even less clear and far less interesting. It is probably associated with *hatching*, not in the chicken-and-egg sense but as in *cross-hatching*, engraving narrow lines on a surface to produce an effect that might, if you squinted at it, look a bit like a hash sign.

A *tag* is a label, formerly a paper one used to identify luggage, for example, or a metal one bearing a soldier's name, blood type and religion; nowadays it is also an electronic one, in computing for marking and identifying the text that follows it, or as a device attached to someone or something (a dog or a criminal, perhaps) for the purposes of monitoring them. Put *hash* and *tag* together and, since the invention of Twitter in the first decade of this century, you have a marker for drawing attention to TWEETs on a specific subject.

icon

If you're referring to the images in the Eastern Orthodox Church, you might spell this *ikon*, but either way it is a painting or other representation of Christ, the Virgin Mary or a saint. This gives it three key aspects that have evolved separately into modern usages. First, it is something to be venerated – and from this idea we get a *pop icon*, someone very much admired (at least for the time being), who could be Miley Cyrus, Madonna or Buddy Holly, depending on your age. Nor are icons confined to the pop world, as long as they are particularly distinguished, innovative or long-lasting in their field: Albert Einstein could be described as *an iconic mathematician*, or Babe Ruth as *an iconic baseball player*. Second, an icon is a symbol, not necessarily a visual one, but a small thing that typifies something larger, such as gospel music and cotton fields being *icons* for the American Deep South. Both of these uses have been around since the 1950s (although they had to wait a while before they could be applied to Miley Cyrus). Third, and most recent, an icon is simply an image or graphic display that you click on to enter an app or operating system. So here we have lost the sense of reverence, which was present in the first two senses, but hung on to the fact that it is a visual representation.

logo

Sir Isaac Pitman's system of shorthand, invented in the 1830s, is based on the concept of representing each spoken sound – rather than each letter – by a distinct symbol. Sir Isaac called these symbols *logograms*, from the Greek for *word* and *letter*. In the news around the same time was a printing system using *logotypes*, blocks of type containing two or more letters such as *on* or *th* that commonly occurred together. Logograms and logotypes seem to have been slightly confused over the course of the next hundred years, with the result that, by the middle of the twentieth century, either term could be applied to a symbol or a form of typography (such as a magazine's masthead) that made a company or a publication readily recognizable. This symbol is, of course, what we now call a *logo* – and as the abbreviation is almost universally used, it doesn't much matter which of the longer words it is short for.

matrix

If you grew up on the Keanu Reeves film you'll be forgiven for thinking that a *matrix* is a simulated and rather malevolent reality; if you're more a *Doctor Who* person you'll assume it is something to do with Jack the Ripper and the evil thoughts of dead Time Lords. In either case you might be surprised to learn that it originally meant the womb – it derives ultimately from *mater*, the Latin for 'mother', just as *maternal* and *maternity* do. A bit of a leap, you might say.

Well, it's not too much of a leap to come from the literal womb in a woman's body to the metaphorical womb in which all sorts of things can be created or can evolve. As early as the sixteenth century you can find idleness being described as the matrix of 'infinite mischiefs' – meaning if you have nothing to do you're likely to get yourself into trouble. Then there are various related meanings in biology, zoology and geology until, by the nineteenth century, you come to 'the set of conditions that make up a particular system', such as the *social matrix*, and, in maths, an arrangement of symbols or expressions in rows and columns.

Skip ahead a hundred years or so and you find the *dot matrix*, also an orderly arrangement, this time of dots or points that can be filled in with ink to produce letters or other symbols on a printout. Another decade – we're into the 1990s now – finds The Matrix with capital letters, 'the global NETWORK of electronic communication', which includes, but is not restricted to, the internet. By the time you get to this definition, The Matrix is big and powerful and potentially scary, so it's not surprising that it should have been adopted by film-makers to describe a dystopian world in which people's minds are imprisoned by an artificial reality.

And you thought it was all about the special effects.

mobile

In its earliest uses in (fifteenth-century) English, *mobile* is a noun, meaning a sphere that orbits the Earth, and an adjective with a similar meaning. The word comes for the Latin for 'movable', as opposed to 'static' or 'fixed in position'.

By the seventeenth century, *mobile* was also short for *mobile vulgus*, the fickle, unreliable common people, easily moved and swayed by a politician's oratory or by the opinion of those around them. This disparaging term was soon further shortened to *mob*.

Later meanings of *mobile*, however, tend to refer to physical movement, not emotional unreliability. The *mobile* that is hung above a baby's cot or pram is so called because its component parts move; the *mobile phone*, a term first recorded as early as 1945, is one that moves around with you rather than sitting in a fixed position in your living room or hall. Americans call this a *cell phone*, for reasons discussed under CELL.

As a counterpoint to a *mobile* or *cell phone*, the term *landline*, sometimes hyphenated and occasionally two words, was coined in the middle of the nineteenth century. In those days it meant 'a telecommunications wire or cable laid over land'. The interpretation most of us would give it nowadays – the fixed-position phone mentioned above, or the number that you use to make it ring – is a twenty-first-century variant, adopted when mobile phones proliferated and what had previously been the norm suddenly needed further explanation.

modem

Well, *modulator demodulator* was never going to catch on, was it? *Modulator*, meaning something that ensured the correct timing of a musical performance, is first found in the sixteenth century; by the early twentieth both it and *demodulator* were being used in the context of physics to refer to devices that helped transmit sound or light signals. The abbreviation *modem* occurs as far back as 1958, although most early references feel the need to define what it means: a 1962 quotation from the *Daily Telegraph* explains, 'The direct current (DC) signals which flow through a computer cannot be transmitted over telephone lines, so it is necessary to convert them ... The black box which does this conversion at either end of the line is called a modem.' In other words, to bring the definition up to date, when you type an email, it is the modem that 'translates' your words into a transmittable signal and then translates them back so that they come out the other end in readable form. Modulating and demodulating them, in fact.

mouse

It's little and it scampers across the floor. Or, in the modern sense, it scampers across a mat and causes your cursor to scamper across your screen. The word was in use in computing circles in the 1960s, though as late as 1982 *The New York Times* felt obliged to explain it by referring to 'a hand-held device known as a mouse'. Most modern laptops now have a trackpad integrated into them; tablets require only your finger; the peripheral plug-in mouse may be departing not so much with a bang as with a barely audible squeak.

netiquette

This is *etiquette* on the *net* – the polite way of behaving in online FORUMS and on social media and the like. First recorded in the 1980s, *netiquette* is defined as an informal code of practice (rather than a strict set of rules), but generally includes such common-sense precautions as 'Don't send a message when you're upset, angry or drunk' and 'Choose an appropriate mode of communication.' That last bit can be translated as 'Don't fire or break up with someone by text message. It isn't nice.'

network

In the Old Testament book of Exodus, God gives Moses detailed instructions (they go on for three chapters) about constructing an ark or tabernacle that will enable the Israelites to carry the divine presence around with them – it becomes known as the Ark of the Covenant. One of the instructions is that the altar inside the ark shall have 'a grate of network of brass' – a grid, in other words, of interwoven bars of brass. I'm quoting the King James Bible, an English translation completed in 1611; this use of *network* in fact goes back to the sixteenth century and it's from this that all the modern senses come. The term *railway network* dates from the earliest days of the railways; *networks of telephone cables*, *television networks* and *computer networks* also emerged as soon as their respective industries required them.

The idea of people *networking* took longer to establish. The *old boy network* so much deplored by those who didn't go to what the British call public and most other nations call private school is first recorded in the 1950s, although the concept doubtless dates back to the invention of public schools. Early uses of *network* to mean 'an interconnected group of people' tend to refer to spies and political organizations; it's only in the 1980s that we find *to network* and *networking* meaning to make a point of meeting useful people and trading favours with them. A lot of business jargon and gobbledygook that has now passed into the language emerged in the 1980s, so the people who first talked about networking were probably also thinking outside the box, indulging in creative accounting and worrying about worst-case scenarios.

pager

In an early scene of the 1935 Marx Brothers' film *A Night at the Opera*, a young man in uniform walks briskly through a hotel dining room calling out, 'Paging

Mr Driftwood, paging Mr Driftwood.' Mr Driftwood (Groucho Marx) stops him and says, 'Do me a favour and stop yelling my name all over this restaurant. Do I go around yelling your name?' – somewhat missing the point of what the *page* was trying to do.

This sense has nothing to do with the *pages* of a book; instead it is connected with the sort of *page* who was in the service of a nobleman back in the day (often in training to become a knight). Part of a page's duties was to carry messages, and this is the sense that transferred itself to American hotels – as a noun around the end of the eighteenth century and as a verb a hundred years later.

Times moved on and by the 1930s if you wanted to contact someone in a hotel or an office, you might use not a pageboy but a public-address system. Fast-forward another thirty years and you have a device, carried perhaps by a doctor on call, that beeps to alert him or her to a message: the *pager*, serving much the same purpose as the boy in uniform, but belonging to an electronic age.

phreak

To phreak is to HACK into a telephone system in order to make calls without paying for them; a person who

does this is also a *phreak*. The word is surprisingly old
– it is first found in the 1970s – and the derivation is
a combination of *phone* and *freak*. This is *freak* in the
slightly disparaging sense found in expressions such
as *health freak* or *fitness freak*: one whose enthusiasm
for a subject verges on the weird.

Some twenty-five years after *phreaking* entered our
consciousness, dishonest people also took to *phishing*.
This means attempting to cheat people by 'fishing'
for information such as their bank details, perhaps by
sending emails that look as if they come from a bona
fide company. The dictionaries say that the word is
an altered spelling of fishing, but the analogy with
phreaking is pretty clear, even though *phishing* is not
usually carried out over the phone.

pixel

A combination of *pix*, the colloquial plural of *pictures*,
and *element*, this adds up to 'the smallest element
with controllable colour and brightness' of which
the image on a computer or television screen is
composed. No one seems to claim credit for coining
the term, but it was in use in the early 1960s.

podcast

This twenty-first-century coinage is a form of audio *broadcast* that is suitable for downloading to an *iPod* or similar media device. The technology was never unique to the iPod; it's just that that massively popular device was ideally suited to it. Probably the first use of the word appeared in a *Guardian* article by Ben Hammersley in February 2004, discussing 'a new boom in amateur radio', which was about to be unleashed by American radio personality Christopher Lydon. 'But what to call it?' Hammersley wondered. 'Audioblogging? Podcasting? GuerillaMedia?' The passage of time has supplied the answer.

programme

The earliest senses of this word and the closely related *programma* are 'an edict, a proclamation' or a similar pronouncement in written form. All the modern but pre-computing meanings arise from this idea of announcing what is going to happen and what form it is going to take: a *programme* can be a course of study or the printed booklet giving details of a play or concert; a *programme of events* gives advance notice of what is to take place on, say, a sports day; a *radio or television programme* puts these events together into a single coherent whole.

Then in the 1940s *programme* (or now almost universally *program*) was adopted to mean the series of operations that a computer could run through – like a *programme of events*, but dealt with automatically. It's a sense that survives when you *programme* the washing machine to deal with the particular garments you want it to wash. But in computing this was soon further adapted to mean not so much the operations as the instructions, the coding or the setting of the switches that told the machine *how* to perform its tasks. Within a very few years the IT world also adopted the word *programmer*. This already existed and meant someone who arranged programmes, whether travel arrangements, sporting events or television broadcasts; now it was applied to the person whose job it was to create *computer programs*.

protocol

The defining factor of a *protocol* in any modern sense is that it is a set of rules. It can mean the parameters laid out at the beginning of a scientific experiment, explaining how that experiment is to be conducted.

It can also be the code of etiquette that surrounds a ceremonial occasion: who sits where, who leaves the room first, that sort of thing. So when, in the 1960s, the computing world needed something to convey 'the set of rules governing the way data is presented so that it can be exchanged between two or more computers', the perfect word was already at hand.

selfie

The OED describes this word as 'originally Australian', and the ending is certainly typical of Aussie slang – think of *tinnie* for a can of beer and *barbie* for a barbecue. Think also of *arvo* for afternoon and *smoko* for a cigarette break and be grateful they decided not to call it a *selfo*: talking about taking a *selfo* on your CELL phone would have twisted tongues from Tasmania to Tuktoyaktuk.

Selfie is an adaptation of *self*, in this case short for *self-portrait* – usually a photographic one taken on a CELL or MOBILE phone or similar device. The first photographic self-portrait was apparently taken by and of the American photographic pioneer Robert Cornelius in 1839, but it was approximately 163 years later that someone Down Under decided to call it a *selfie*. Such is the speed of development of modern technology and terminology, though, that it was a mere eleven years after that, in 2013, that the OED designated *selfie* as its 'word of the year'. Given that recent 'words of the year' have included *chav*, *unfriend* and *squeezed middle*, it's a matter of opinion how much of a compliment this is.

server

In addition to earlier meanings connected with waiting at table and with tennis, a *server* is a PROGRAM that manages shared access to a centralized resource in a NETWORK, storing communal files, processing email and so on; it can also be the machine on which these functions are performed.

Servers of one sort or another have been around for hundreds of years: they were people who served food from the fifteenth century; the players who put the ball into play from the sixteenth; plates from which food was served from the seventeenth; a spoon and fork used to serve salad from the nineteenth; and machines or the programs that run them from the late twentieth. All providing a service in their own way.

spam

Considering how much of an acquired taste it is, Spam has been remarkably popular. It's a sort of canned lunch meat and was launched in 1937 by the Hormel Foods Corporation, boasting the twin advantages of being cheap and having a much longer shelf-life than fresh meat. Hormel shipped over 100 million pounds (about 45 million kilos) of Spam abroad to feed allied troops during the Second World War, and over the years they have produced over seven billion cans, with various different flavours including 'hickory smoke', 'with cheese chunks' and a low-fat, low-sodium version. Someone must be eating it.

The story goes that Hormel wanted a catchy name for the new product and ran a competition. It was won by an actor called Kenneth Daigneau, who was also, according to some versions, the brother of one of the company's vice presidents. The normal explanation is that spam is short for 'spiced ham'; the idea that it was an acronym for Something Posing As Meat was surely made up by jaundiced soldiers who felt they had eaten too much of it.

Then in 1970 a sketch in the television comedy *Monty Python's Flying Circus* featured a café in which nearly everything on the menu contained Spam. Most explanations of the origin of *spam* as the name for junk advertising via email cite the *Python* sketch as having introduced the idea that spam got everywhere and nobody wanted it.

switch

In the seventeenth century a *switch* was a thin, flexible twig, often used as a whip, and flexibility is the quality that is required of a modern switch. Whether it's on a railway, used to shunt a train from one line to another; or an *electrical switch* for operating a light or a power socket; or a *switch-blade knife* on which you press a button to shoot the blade out of its sheath, the point is that you press a switch up or down, in or out, and by doing so you make something change direction or turn it on or off. These various uses developed as the need for them arose, from the late eighteenth century onwards.

tablet

In American English a *tablet* is still what it has been for 150 years – what the British call a writing pad or notepad. This meaning derives directly from the original one – a stiff, wax-covered sheet for writing on, used in Ancient Rome and in Europe up to the Middle Ages. When writing in wax you used not a pen but a stylus, which enabled you to etch your words into the surface. That is substantially what happens with a modern *tablet* – you can use a smooth-ended stylus to 'click' on the on-screen keyboard when Tweeting or to move your video-game character through its VIRTUAL world. Essentially, the concept of the tablet is exactly what it has always been: a small, hand-held, flattish device on which you can make your mark. Only now it is a computer.

See also STILETTO and TABLOID.

technocracy

Words ending in *-cracy* (forming an abstract noun) or *-crat* (denoting a person) are to do with ruling or government: *democracy* is government by the people, *aristocracy* was originally government by the best people and even today, despite what other people may think, an *aristocrat* is likely to categorize himself as one of the best. Both these concepts existed in Ancient Greece and the words were in use in English by the sixteenth century. *Bureaucracy*, government by officials – particularly tedious, paper-pushing,

more-than-my-job's-worth-to-bend-the-rules officials
– appeared in English in the early nineteenth, having
been adopted from a French word that had emerged
half a century before, *bureaucratie*. (It seems that
from the earliest times *bureaucracy* had a bad name:
the eighteenth-century French economist Jacques de
Gournay, credited with coining the term, complained
of a national 'illness' he called *bureaumania*, which
'bids fair to play havoc with us'.)

Technocracy – government by *technocrats* or
scientific and technical experts – is a newer concept,
but perhaps older than you might expect. William
Henry Smyth, an American consulting engineer
and inventor, claimed to have coined it in an
article published in 1919. He was writing about an
experiment in 'rationalized Industrial Democracy',
which was carried out 'by organizing and co-
ordinating the Scientific Knowledge, the Technical
Talent, the Practical Skill and the Man Power of the
entire Community: focusing them in the National
Government, and applying this Unified National Force
to the accomplishment of a Unified National Purpose'.
This is what he described as *technocracy*. However,
an 1895 edition of the *Economic Journal*, quoted by
the OED, refers to '"technocracy" in the history of
medicine' and shows that the word was around a
generation before Smyth's experiment. Even so, he
seems to have given it a new lease of life and it soon

passed into more common use, with *technocrat* and *technocratic* hard on its heels.

troll

If you know the fairy tale of the 'Three Billy Goats Gruff', you'll probably remember that the evil being who lurked beneath the bridge and threatened anyone trying to cross it was a *troll*. It was in the version I read as a child, anyway. There is a Polish version where the villain is a wolf, but that needn't concern us here. This sort of *troll* comes from Norse mythology and is a bad-tempered, ugly creature, formerly a giant, now usually a dwarf. There's another, unrelated word *troll* whose meanings have to do with going to and fro in a repetitive way, perhaps trying to provoke a reaction. The recent unpleasant creation, *the internet troll* – someone who deliberately posts antagonistic or abusive messages in the hope of sparking a response – is probably a mixture of the two.

tweet

The social networking site Twitter was launched in 2006 and now has over a hundred million users worldwide. At the time of writing, and using the roundest of round figures, this means it has acquired an average of 30,000 users per day since Day One. Not bad.

One of the founders, Jack Dorsey, is quoted as explaining the name thus:

> ... We came across the word 'twitter', and it was just perfect. The definition was 'a short burst of inconsequential information' and 'chirps from birds'. And that's exactly what the product was.

Just in case you aren't one of the site's hundred million users, the idea is that you send messages of no more than 140 characters (including spaces and punctuation). That's perhaps twenty words. It may well be that Twitter contains a lot of inconsequential information, but at least it is brief inconsequential information.

The message – as at least a hundred million people in the world are aware – is called a *tweet*, which for a couple of centuries before that had meant the high chirping sound of a small bird. It still does mean that, but for how long? And what will the birds do when someone invents a social networking site called Chirrup?

virtual

Given what the word means nowadays, it's perhaps surprising to think that *virtual* was originally an adjective deriving from *virtue* and referred to powerful natural qualities. The British author Richard Ligon, living in Barbados in the seventeenth century, described 'the *virtual* beams of the Sun' as giving 'growth and life to all the Plants and Flowers it shines on', which sounds very odd if you interpret *virtual* in any modern sense. At the same time, however, *virtual* meant what it continued to mean for several hundred years – 'in effect, potentially', the opposite of *real* or *actual*.

That, of course, is where the modern meaning comes from: something that exists or takes place online or via the internet, rather than having a solid, physical being. Thus you can have *virtual musical instruments* – software that enables you to compose, play and produce a sound like the real thing; *virtual colleges*, which enable you to learn and obtain qualifications without attending a bricks-and-mortar institution; *virtual tours* of museums, stately homes and properties for sale, which you can take without leaving your couch; and of course *virtual reality*, a computer-generated simulation of a real environment.

This may be great fun for players of video games and immensely useful training for astronauts or racing drivers, but in a linguistic context *virtual reality* is surely the ultimate contradiction in terms. Be that as it may, the expression has been around since the 1970s, has superseded *variant reading* and *Victoria Regina* as what most people think *VR* stands for, and gives you almost 54 million hits on Google if you type in just those two words. It's not going away any time soon.

virus

In medical terms, a *virus* is a pathogenic (disease-causing) agent that can replicate itself rapidly within a living organism; it's also popularly used to refer to the disease caused by such an agent. The common cold is caused by a virus; if you weren't sure what was wrong with you, you might also say that you had 'picked up a BUG'.

So there are two key points here: a virus is a bad thing and it spreads rapidly. Both of which are exactly what *computer viruses* do. In a paper produced in 1984, the American computer scientist Frederick B. Cohen gave the first published definition: a virus, he explained, is 'a PROGRAM that can "infect" other programs by modifying them to include a possibly evolved copy of itself ... a virus can spread throughout a computer system or network using the authorizations of every user using it to infect their programs. Every program that gets infected may also act as a virus and thus the infection grows.'

The speed with which a virus spreads and the knock-on effect of one thing infecting another were given a different application in the 1990s when the concept of *viral marketing* emerged. The thinking was that, once one person liked an idea or a product, he or she would mention it to someone else, who would mention it to someone else again, or, if really enthusiastic, email it to everyone in their address book. In other words, the news would spread like what used to be called wildfire. When social media came into being, the spreading became even quicker, with the result that a few seconds of film of, say, a politician making an idiot of himself, could *go viral* – notching up millions of views on YouTube – in a terrifyingly short space of time.

watch

When the name *watch* was first applied to a timepiece, five or six hundred years ago, it referred not to the small but decorative thing you wear on your wrist but to an alarm clock. Earlier senses of the word are to do with wakefulness and alertness, as in *keeping watch* or *the watches of the night*. Thus the first timekeeping *watches* were intended to wake you up and perhaps, if you were on a ship, to warn you that it was your turn to be on *watch duty*.

Portable timepieces, originally worn round the neck as pendants, were being made in Germany in the sixteenth century; Queen Elizabeth I's favourite the Earl of Leicester gave her a present of an early 'arm watch' in 1571. Watches for the wrist remained a largely female accessory until a hundred years ago: men tended to use pocket watches or, from the nineteenth century, to wear their watch on a chain clipped to the front of the waistcoat – a device made fashionable by Queen Victoria's husband and therefore known as an *albert*. By this time, the idea that a watch's principal function was to wake you up was firmly in the past, but the name remained the same.

web

Dictionary definitions of the World Wide Web are scary, referring as they do to documents being stored at numerous locations worldwide and accessed by hypertext PROTOCOLS. But we all know what the

Web is – it's that thing that is magically there at our fingertips when we turn our computer on and tells us everything we want to know about train times, eBay and definitions of the World Wide Web. It was first proposed by Tim Berners-Lee at a conference at CERN (the European Organization for Nuclear Research) in 1989, and its initial purpose was to facilitate the sharing of information between scientists at various universities and institutes across the world. At around the same time, the *interconnecting networks* or *internets* that had linked various smaller computer networks took their first tentative steps towards world domination, and acquired an initial capital letter.

The very first *website* (a word coined in the early 1990s) was in fact dedicated to the World Wide Web and consisted of a single, unillustrated page with a number of links to such things as an executive summary, technical details, policy and, endearingly at this early stage, Frequently Asked Questions. Although Berners-Lee used the abbreviation W3, this first website also refers to *the web*.

The name seems to have been chosen because the web got rid of the frustration of incompatible formats, meaning that anything could link up to anything, the way that threads do in a spider's web. One of the other options, The Information Mesh (which would have abbreviated to the inventor's first name), may have been rejected because it looked too like The Information Mess.

Another characteristic of a spider's web, of course, is that the unsuspecting are caught in it and ensnared for evermore, but that's probably a coincidence.

webinar

This neat linking of *web* and *seminar* produces a seminar conducted via the internet. Thanks to the miracle of modern video-conferencing software, participants can join in discussions with fellow students and with the tutor – who may be on another continent – without leaving home or the office. As with many terms connected with business, this originated in the US; it was first used in the 1990s.

zoom

The first uses of *zoom* refer to the noise it makes: it was originally (in the late nineteenth century) a verb meaning to emit a low humming or buzzing sound. Because anything making that sort of noise was likely to be travelling rapidly, the word quickly acquired a sense of speed, too: by the 1920s the *British Weekly* was able to write about trams (also known as trolley cars) *zooming along* and buses rattling past. (People were more easily impressed in those days – I can't imagine any modern tram hitting a speed that could be described as *zooming*.)

During the First World War, aircraft slang adopted *zoom* and adapted it to mean climbing briefly at a sharp angle, hence the figurative idea of prices *zooming*. Then by the 1930s the photographic and motion picture worlds needed a word to describe a shot that moved quickly into close-up without going out of focus. That sort of *zoom* required a *zoom lens* to *zoom in* on its subject and a new piece of photographic gadgetry – and jargon – was born.

CHAPTER FOUR

A Transport of Delight

Humans have been travelling from Point A to Point B since time immemorial. The changes in vocabulary come about when Point B becomes that much farther from Point A (it may even be somewhere in space) and when we learn to get there in different and faster ways. This chapter also looks at some of the places we stay on our travels.

caravan

You know those pictures of a line of camels trudging through the desert, one after the other, as if they didn't have a thought in their heads other than to follow the camel in front? That's a *caravan*. Or, strictly speaking, it isn't the camels so much as the people with them, travelling in a group for the sake of security. The word was adapted into English from the Persian around 1600.

When people started exploring the Wild West of America, they too travelled in groups for security and used the same term. It wasn't long before caravan came to be applied not only to the convoy but to the individual horse-drawn wagons that composed it, and from there to other covered wagons, such as those used by gypsies and circus folk.

But these caravans were all used for serious purposes: either trail-blazing travel, business or day-to-day living. The caravan as the British know it – a vehicle for leisure purposes – was pioneered by a Scottish writer named William Gordon Stables, who in the 1880s commissioned the Bristol Waggon Works to build him a covered wagon (or perhaps a waggon) to be drawn by two horses. He named it The Wanderer, took it on a lengthy tour of Scotland and wrote about his travels in a book called *The Cruise of the Land-Yacht Wanderer, Or Thirteen Hundred*

Miles in My Caravan. Stables' adventures sparked something of a craze for *caravanning* among those who could afford it, and when car ownership became widespread after the First World War it seemed only sensible to invent something that served the same purpose and could be towed along behind the car – and to give it the same name.

Incidentally, *van* – the vehicle in which such things as furniture are delivered – is a contraction of *caravan*. It's not to be confused with *in the van* meaning *in the forefront*. This is short for *vanguard*, from the French *avant garde*, meaning 'advance guard'. So one sort of van is by definition in the front; the other is short for something that is towed behind. Confusing, but just one of those things.

chauffeur

The French verb *chauffer* means to heat and in French in the days of steam trains *chauffeur* could mean a fireman or stoker, as well as a driver. A modern French *chauffeur* might be driving a bus or a lorry rather than a car – it means simply 'the person who happens to be driving'. When the word was first adopted into English at the turn of the twentieth century it had that broader sense, but as early as

1902 the fact that the word was French had given it a certain cachet among the élite. In that year the *Westminster Gazette* was able to report that, in the quest to find a word to designate a paid, professional driver, '"chauffeur" seems at present to hold the field'. As, indeed, it has done ever since.

express

The French word *exprès* means 'on purpose, deliberately' and in English *express* had a similar meaning for several hundred years; we still use the adverb in this way, as in *it was produced expressly for the occasion*. So the original *express trains* weren't designed for speed, necessarily, but for a purpose: a *special* (or *express*) TRAIN might be commissioned to take crowds to a race meeting or to the coast in the summer. But because such a train was heading for a particular destination and not stopping at the usual intermediate STATIONS, it got there more quickly than it would normally have done.

The original *Orient Express* may well have been special, but it certainly wasn't speedy: for the first six years of its service (1883–9), passengers for Constantinople (now Istanbul) had to do part of the journey by ferry or by horse-drawn carriage. Even when the railway line across Bulgaria was completed in 1889, the whole trip from Paris to Constantinople took sixty-seven and a half hours.

Even so, by the end of the nineteenth century, the word *express* was being used with reference to other appliances and services where speed was implicit: *express delivery* of mail, an *express rifle* and, not longer afterwards, an *express elevator* that didn't stop at every floor. By the 1930s and 1940s, the Americans had also invented the *express highway* or *expressway,* designed specifically (or expressly) for fast-moving traffic.

hitch

There was no need for the word *hitchhike* until the 1920s, when for the first time a significant number of people owned a motor car and others – mostly the impoverished young – took to travelling farther from home than they had ever done before, relying on the kindness of strangers for lifts. The original meaning of *hitch* was to move jerkily or unevenly – a perfect description of a journey where you have to get out of the car when the driver has reached his or her own destination, then walk (or *hike*) a bit farther until someone else picks you up. *Hitchhike* had been abbreviated to *hitch* – as in *to hitch a lift* or *a ride* – within a very few years.

Hike itself is a surprisingly recent coinage – early nineteenth century – of uncertain derivation. It initially carried the implication of walking for pleasure and came into being when a growing middle class started doing just that. Before this time, walking was something you were obliged to do because you weren't rich enough to own your own carriage or pay the fare on a stagecoach: very few people did it for the fun of it.

jet

Etymologically connected with *jut* and *jetty*, this neat little word originally meant something that sticks out, a projection. From this, in the seventeenth century, it was applied to a stream of water or gas, propelled forward or upwards – so you might have a *jet of steam* pouring from a fast-boiling kettle. Harnessing that power produces *jet propulsion*, which in turn can drive a *jet engine*.

Despite the fact that this principle powers the world's most impressive aircraft, you don't need much grasp of physics to understand how it works. The website of aircraft manufacturer Boeing gives this straightforward explanation:

A jet engine uses a gas turbine to drive a fan that sucks in air, mixes it with burning fuel, and then blasts the expanded air-gas mixture out the back. Because every action has an equal and opposite reaction, as the air streams backward the engine is forced forward.

The first jet engines were developed in the 1920s; *jet aircraft* were used during the Second World War and were abbreviated to *jet* before the end of it. Then the first commercial *jet,* the de Havilland Comet, made its debut on a BOAC flight from London to Johannesburg in 1952 and the planes and the word were here to stay.

The original *jumbo jet* was the Boeing 747, launched at the end of the 1960s and given its nickname because of its vast size: its capacity of about 500 passengers was two and a half times that of its predecessor, the 737.

juggernaut

There can't be many vehicles that derive their names from Hindu gods, but the *juggernaut* is one of them. Juggernaut or Jagannath (meaning 'lord of the world') is one of the many titles of the god Krishna, who is himself an avatar of the supreme god Vishnu. Juggernaut is worshipped in the Indian city of Puri, where a temple dating back to the twelfth century houses an image of him as an odd-looking creature with bulging eyes, a blood-red mouth and no limbs.

So how does he come to have a type of heavy truck named after him? Well, every year the citizens of Puri place the image of Jagannath on a heavy chariot and process it through the streets. Thousands of pilgrims crowd around and are occasionally crushed under the vehicle's wheels. And not only by accident. One Friar Odoric, a witness to the festival in the fourteenth century, reported that worshippers 'cast themselves under the chariot, so that its wheels may go over them, saying that they desire to die for their god'. It's from this extreme form of devotion that we get the idea of a *juggernaut* as something that demands utter self-sacrifice or as an overwhelmingly dominant institution, such as a government department, that moves ruthlessly and inflexibly along its own path, destroying anything that stands in its way. From that image to the idea of a similarly implacable truck requires only a small stretch of the imagination.

long-haul

What's interesting here is the *haul* part: it comes from the word you'd expect it to come from, the one that means *to drag* or *to tug*. As a noun, *a haul* is the distance over which something is hauled: from the seventeenth century it described the catch that was picked up in a fishing net dragged along behind a boat; from the nineteenth it was also used in logging and other industries where the product had to be dragged from source to point of delivery. *Long* (or *short*) *haul* was also used figuratively: 'We're in it for the long haul' meant 'We aren't expecting instant results and we aren't going to give up easily.'

All these senses still exist, but from the early days of long-distance aeroplane journeys – the 1950s – both *long-haul* and *short-haul* have come to be applied to air travel. Now the commodity being *hauled* is people and the difference between the two is whether they are crossing continents or just flying for a couple of hours for a meeting or a weekend break.

minibus

The first London *omnibuses* were introduced on a route between Paddington and the Bank in 1829; they were designed to carry twenty-two passengers and were drawn by three horses. The idea and the name had been brought over from Paris, where they had for ten years been providing cheap urban transport for those who couldn't afford their own carriage.

The Latin word *omnibus* means 'for everyone'. *Omnis* means 'all' and *–ibus* is the inflection indicating 'for'. So to abbreviate *omnibus* to *bus* may have been convenient but was surely frowned on by anyone with a knowledge of Latin (which in those days meant practically everyone who had been to school for more than a year or two). Nevertheless, the word *bus* appeared almost as soon as the vehicle itself. And when, in 1832, a *cabriolet* (the source of the modern word *cab*) designed to carry only two passengers hit the London streets, it was nicknamed 'the omnibus slice', 'the duobus' or 'the *minibus*'.

Minibus fell into abeyance when these horse-drawn carriages ceased to be a feature of our city streets, but *omnibus* transferred itself to its motorized equivalent. Soon only the most diehard of pedants would have frowned on the word *bus* (though some would still have insisted on spelling it *'bus*). So in the 1950s it made perfect sense that a new vehicle, designed to carry about a third of the number of passengers of the standard modern bus, should be called a *minibus*.

motel

This word has been so familiar to holidaymakers for so long that it's easy to overlook the fact that it started life as *motor hotel* – a hotel that you drove to and that, unlike many old-fashioned urban or coastal hotels, had ample parking space. *Motel* was coined in the 1920s, in plenty of time for Norman Bates' establishment in *Psycho* to be – at first glance, at least – an unthreatening roadside haven. By analogy, *botel* or *boatel* emerged in the 1950s as a place catering to boat-owners, who could have the twin pleasures of sailing by day and sleeping at night in a bed that wasn't prone to pitching and tossing.

motorcade

Purists will tell you that a *cavalcade* must contain horses, because the first part of the word harks back to the Latin *caballus*, meaning a horse, and *caballicare*, to ride a horse. Meaning 'a procession on horseback', *cavalcade* dates back to at least the seventeenth century, but was adapted to include a more varied sort of procession – including carriages or other vehicles – by the eighteenth. If you look at *caballicare*, though, you'll deduce that the horsey part of the word *cavalcade* is *cavalc–*; *–ade* is the suffix denoting an

action, as in *escapade* or *cannonade.* So when, in the
early twentieth century, somebody decided that a
procession containing motor vehicles should be called
a *motorcade*, that somebody was clearly not a Latin
scholar. Probably just as well, though, as *motorade,*
despite being more linguistically correct, would
have sounded like a car-based idea for a charitable
fundraising event (see *telethon* under TELEGENIC), or
perhaps a soft drink that you drank only while driving.

plane

In geometry a *plane* is a flat surface on which a
straight line joining any two points will fully lie. This
technical term was adopted into the word *aéroplane*,
coined in 1855 by a Frenchman named Joseph Pline:
it was the name he gave to his proposed 'dirigible
glider' on the basis that it was somewhat flatter than
earlier flying devices (many of which were balloons).
The word was quickly taken into English, where the
original *aeroplane* was not the flying machine itself
but the more or less flat wings used to lift it. As the
concept of powered flight developed, *aeroplane* came
to be used for any heavier-than-air aircraft, whatever
its shape, although *airplane* was officially preferred in
the USA as early as 1916.

Aeroplane was being abbreviated to *plane* (or, by the meticulous, *'plane*) in the first decade of the twentieth century, thereby ditching the part of the word that had made an aeroplane (or an airplane) unusual in the first place.

On a par with an aeroplane are an *aquaplane*, something that skims along the surface of the water, and an *aerofoil* or *airfoil*, a structure providing lift to an aircraft, or improving road-holding ability on a motor vehicle. The *foil* part derives from the Latin for *leaf* and refers to its shape and its slimness. Both these words date from the early twentieth century; a decade or so later we were putting similar useful word elements together and coming up with the *hydrofoil* – based on the Greek for water, instead of the Latin *aqua*. It served much the same purpose as an aerofoil but was used on ships and seaplanes and had its effect when travelling through water rather than air.

post

In his account of the civil war he fought against Pompey the Great in the first century BC, Julius Caesar wrote about having horsemen – and more importantly horses – stationed at regular intervals along a strategic route. It meant that one messenger could pass news, whether written or verbal, to another, who then went speeding off on the next stage of the journey. News could travel much more quickly if its transmission didn't depend on a single rider, who had to stop every hour or so to rest his horse. Caesar's word for 'stationed' is *dispositos*, which ultimately derives from the Latin verb for *to place*, *to position* or, if you prefer, *to post*.

Various parts of Europe picked up on this idea, and by the fifteenth century the places where spare horses were available became known as *posts*. *Posting inns* maintained stables so that coaches could change horses without delay to their journey. In the sixteenth century the verb *to post* meant to travel from *post* to *post* – changing horses when necessary – and also to travel quickly, hence the expression *post haste*.

Initially the only person in England allowed to send messages via this *postal system* was the monarch. However, in the seventeenth century this right was extended to private individuals and in 1660 Charles II established the General *Post Office*, with a network of branches where letters or parcels could be deposited for forwarding to a specified recipient. The nineteenth-century novelist Anthony Trollope, who worked for the Post Office for many years, is credited with the invention of the *post-box* which still adorns British streets: thanks to him, you no longer had to go to the Post Office in order to post a letter.

Long before Trollope's day, however, *post* had acquired a specialist meaning in bookkeeping: from the seventeenth century you *posted* entries into a ledger to keep a record of monies spent or received. When computing spreadsheets came along in the late twentieth century, the same term was adopted and accountants started *posting data*. Then came internet FORUMS, BLOGS and social media, enabling the lay person to *post opinions*; it was only logical to call the thing being posted a *post*.

Much of this usage, of course, is predominantly British. Many other English-speaking countries send letters not via the post but via the *mail*. This comes from an Old French word for a travelling bag and by the seventeenth century meant specifically a bag in which a courier carried messages. From this it was a short step to using *mail* to refer to the messages themselves and also to the vehicle – a *mail coach* and later a *mail train* – that carried them. Like so many things in American history, the creation of a Post Office can be attributed to Benjamin Franklin (see BATTERY). The US Constitution empowers Congress 'to establish post offices and post roads' and the United States Post Office Department was established in 1792, to be superseded by the United States Postal Service in 1971. But no one outside the realm of officialdom calls this body anything other than the US Mail and when, in 1968, Elvis Presley sang about 'not tampering with the property of the US Male', everybody understood the pun.

In the twenty-first century, of course, since so much of our *mail* has become *electronic*, the word is used universally in a new context.

satellite

The Latin *satelles* meant an attendant, companion or accomplice and *satellite* appears in fourteenth-century French with a similar meaning – a courtier or attendant in the retinue of an important person. In the early seventeenth century Galileo Galilei discovered the four largest moons of Jupiter (as did his lesser known rival, Simon Marius, a subject about which there was bitter dispute among astronomers). It was a third astronomer, Johannes Kepler, an admirer of Galileo, who first called them *satellites*, although the individual names by which they are known to this day – Io, Callisto, Ganymede and Europa, all objects of Jupiter or Zeus's desire in classical mythology – were Marius's idea.

Moons, of course, orbit planets or other celestial bodies, as courtiers revolve round their monarch. So when, in the 1950s, manmade objects were sent into space to orbit the earth, it made sense to call them satellites too. *Communications satellites* sent out the signals for *satellite television*, which required a *satellite dish* to receive its signals, though neither the television nor the dish was obliged to do any orbiting.

The first manmade satellite was a Russian *sputnik* – literally a travelling companion, with the *–nik* suffix denoting a member of a class or group. Although *sputnik* isn't used in English in anything other than the space-race sense, *–nik* was adopted to create such 1960s words as *beatnik,* a member of the 'beat generation', and *peacenik*, a supporter of peace and specifically one who objected to Western participation in the Vietnam War. As the Cold War between West and East was rumbling on at the same time, it has been suggested that the largely American use of a Russian suffix contributed to the disapproval inherent in these words.

shuttle

Long before weaving was done by machines, a *shuttle* was a handheld instrument used to pass the weft threads back and forth across the warp ones, interlacing the two to form a fabric. In the eighteenth century, an inventor called John Kay came up with a much speedier version known as the 'flying shuttle' and the Industrial Revolution was on its way.

The point about a shuttle, whether mechanized or not, was that it went backwards and forwards over a short distance. So, in the 1890s, what better word to apply to a railway service that did the same thing? And later to other similar forms of transport. It's appealing, I think, that the weaver's shuttle was often boat-shaped, so in French it was called a *navette*, from the word for a ship. In modern French the same word is used for a *shuttle service* which, if it is crossing the English Channel, is quite likely to *be* a ship. In order to produce this naval-sounding name, therefore, the word went from shipping to weaving and back again.

sleeper

Meaning simply a person who sleeps well, or who sleeps too much and is lazy and unproductive, this word can be found in *The Canterbury Tales* (*c.* 1386) and indeed in Middle English works a century and more before that. In more modern English it has various uses to do with sleeping – it can mean the sleeping car on a TRAIN, for instance, or a suit for a baby to sleep in or a spy who lurks in the background for a long time before going into action – but from there to a piece of timber to support the rails of a railway seems quite a leap.

The explanation lies in the stationary nature of such timbers. As far back as the fifteenth century, in general building a *dormant timber* or *dormant tree* was one that was fixed in position, unable to move; by the beginning of the eighteenth *sleeper* was used with roughly this meaning – a heavy beam that supported other parts of the structure. The term could also be used in ship-building and was adopted when the same principle was needed in the burgeoning railways. Vital though these support beams were and are, the name seems to have come from the fact that sleepers were usually horizontal, so they appeared to be lying around not doing very much.

Sleeper meaning a small earring used to keep the holes in pierced ears open is similarly unkind. It is, like a sleeper in building, performing a useful task, but a temporary and rather passive one. If the function of an earring is to be flashy and eye-catching, then the unobtrusive sleeper is, to all intents and purposes, just lying there.

station

From the Latin for *to stand*, this word has existed for seven hundred years in the sense of 'an allocated position, the place from which you do your duty'. It's still used, mostly in North America, for the group of tables assigned to an individual waiter. For almost as long, it has meant an army garrison ('the troops were *stationed* at X Camp') or, as *a naval station*, the equivalent 'home base' for ships. When Christians started going out into the world to convert the supposedly irreligious, they established *mission stations*; and someone who was excessively interested in what her neighbours were up to might *take up a* (metaphorical) *station* at the window to watch passers-by.

So the word was well established when first transport systems and then broadcasting companies came along and needed a term to describe their own bases. Both *railway stations* and *bus stations* appeared in the 1830s; *radio stations* followed in the early twentieth century.

See also CHANNEL and TERMINUS.

staycation

Short for '*stay*-at-home *vacation*', this portmanteau was coined in the early years of this century, when economic problems encouraged first Americans and then Brits to have a holiday at home. It can mean either going out during the day and returning to sleep in your own bed (thus spending a fair bit on travel but saving on accommodation) or having a holiday in your home country (saving on PLANE fares). You pays your money – though hopefully a bit less than usual – and you takes your choice.

tarmac

The Scottish engineer John Loudon McAdam (1756–1836) invented a method of surfacing roads that made them more durable and less prone to getting carriages stuck in them in bad weather (always a worry with the soil-based tracks that had been the norm until then). His method – which became known as *macadamization*, despite the fact that he spelled his name without an *a* in the first syllable – consisted of covering compacted subsoil with small pieces of broken stone, all of the same size. These would be compacted in their turn before being covered by a second layer. The result was a smooth, hard surface. Charles Darwin was familiar with this method: when he visited Australia in the late 1830s he recorded approvingly that roads leading inland from Sydney were 'excellent, and made upon the MacAdam principle: whinstone having been brought for the purpose from the distance of several miles'.

By the 1880s other inventive people had improved on McAdam's original recipe, notably by adding tar and creosote to the stone – a concoction known as *tar macadam* (sometimes one word, sometimes hyphenated). Then in 1902 a Welsh-born engineer named Edgar Purnell Hooley patented a product he called Tarmac. Hooley's proprietary name, now usually written without the initial capital, came to be used for any similar road-surfacing material and indeed for the area it covered, such as a roadway or airport runway. John Loudon McAdam would have every reason to be pleased to see how widely his invention and his carelessly spelled name had spread.

terminus

This is Latin for 'end' or 'boundary'; the Ancient Romans had a god called Terminus who looked after landmarks and was embodied in boundary stones. So, in the eighteenth century, a *terminus* could mean anything that marked a boundary. It could also mean any end point or goal – and even, occasionally and perversely, a starting point. Thus in the nineteenth century it was a useful word for the new concept of a STATION that marked the end of a railway line. The difference, then as now, was that a *station* could be anywhere along the line; the *terminus* was by definition at the end – or, of course, at the beginning, when the TRAIN turned round and went back in the other direction.

train

The origins of this word are complex. They involve dragging something or someone along behind you, like the *train* of a bride's dress or the *train* (of people) that accompanies an exalted personage. But this sense is mingled with the idea of a sequence or course, as in *a train of thought*, and of guiding something in the right direction, as in *training a plant* or an athlete being *in training*.

The modern *railway train* comes from a merging of all these meanings, but perhaps lays most emphasis on the idea of one thing following another: in this context, *train* originally designated a number of cars or carts coupled together in a mine, to carry the extracted mineral to the surface. From the late eighteenth century, such cars were drawn along narrow-gauge railways built for the purpose, drawn sometimes by men and boys, sometimes by pit ponies and later by steam or electricity.

In the early nineteenth century, the word *train*

was applied to the overground public conveyance we know today, but strictly speaking it meant the linked row of carriages or wagons that followed the engine. By 1825, however, it had drifted into a more general sense, to cover the whole 'unit', engine and all. So nowadays it is possible (but etymologically inaccurate) to describe a little cross-country service that consists of only one car as a *train*.

Oddly, too, you could describe the people in a monarch or president's *train* as SATELLITES, although purists would purse their lips and tell you that *trains* followed behind their luminary and *satellites* orbited around.

tube

A *tube* is a long, hollow body, usually cylindrical, used to contain something (such as toothpaste) or, especially in a biological sense, to allow something to pass from one part of the body to another (such as eggs along the *Fallopian tubes*). Although the first part of the London Underground dates from 1863, the name *Tube* didn't become established until 1900, when the Central London Railway – from Ealing Broadway to Liverpool Street, serving many of the stations on today's Central Line – opened. The fare on this line was twopence, no matter how far you were going, and the service quickly became known at the Twopenny Tube. At first the *Tube* meant only the tunnel through which the *Tube Railway* passed, but the name soon came to encompass both the trains and the entire NETWORK.

The term Underground, as anyone who travels to Farringdon or Barons Court, for example, will know, is something of a misnomer, as less than half of London's Underground system is underground. The same objection could be made to the New York *subway* – literally something that goes under (*sub*) the *roadway* or *railway*; in New York some 40 per cent of the subway system isn't underground, and part of it is actually elevated. Nevertheless, *subway* was in use in this context as early as the 1850s and is still the official term for the Glasgow Underground system, but is confusing to Londoners who often have to walk along long *subways* (underground passages) to get to the Tube.

Metro – used in Paris since 1900 and in much of the rest of Europe – is short for *metropolitan*, itself an abbreviation for the name of the original operator, the *Paris Metropolitan Railway Company*. The modern Paris Metropolitan Area extends beyond the furthest reaches of the Metro, making its name the most accurate of the three.

CHAPTER FIVE

Politics, Business and Science

This is a bit of a catch-all section ranging from ether to kettling, and from dental floss to tanks. It's interesting to note that quite a few of the words dealing with politics and the business world started as terms of abuse or mockery – so no change there.

bear

On the stock exchange, a *bear market* is one where prices are falling. In the early eighteenth century, a *bearskin jobber* sold stock he did not possess at an agreed price; assuming prices then fell quickly, he could buy at a lower price, deliver the stock to his customer without undue delay and make a handsome profit on the deal. (In the Wall Street Crash of 1929 this was known as 'selling short' and was regarded as very canny or very dodgy, depending on your moral standpoint.) *Bearskin jobber* was shortened to *bear*, denoting either the stock traded in this way or the person who traded it. Richard Steele, writing in the *Tatler* in 1709, explained it thus: 'I fear the Word Bear is hardly to be understood among the polite People; but I take the meaning to be, That one who ensures a Real Value upon an Imaginary Thing, is said to sell a Bear.' The OED suggests that the expression was associated with the proverb 'Don't sell the bearskin before you have killed the bear', a practice closely related to counting your chickens before they are hatched.

The opposite of this is a *bull market*, a term coined shortly after *bear*. In Charles Johnson's highly successful comedy *The Country Lasses* (1714), a character bemoaning the fact that London has gone to the dogs says that, 'Instead of changing honest staple for Gold and Silver, you deal in Bears and Bulls only; you have Women who are chaste, and would yet appear lewd; and you have Saints that are Sinners; in short 'tis a very wicked Town.' Johnson clearly expected his audience to understand what he meant, suggesting that the rising *bull market* was already an established concept.

board

The earliest meaning for this multi-faceted word is a flat piece of timber – a sense that dates back a thousand years and more. It quickly evolved to mean a table made of such a piece of timber, and from that became the food and drink served at a table – as in *board and lodging* or *bed and board*. But other things can happen round a table; one of them is a meeting. Thus a council or other officially appointed group of people came, by the seventeenth century, to be known as a *board*: Shakespeare refers to an 'honourable board of council' in one of his last plays, *Henry VIII*. The first mention of a *board of directors* appears in the early eighteenth century; a hundred years later Dickens' *Sketches by Boz* have a poor woman appearing before the *parish board* in their *board room*.

Although we still use *board* to mean a piece of wood, this original meaning is now so far removed in our minds from the *boardroom* that there is no oddity about sitting around the *boardroom table.* But, if you think about it, it really is a bit odd.

boom

It's not certain where the use of this word to describe a period of economic prosperity came from, but the most common suggestion is that it is connected with the older (but still current) sense of *boom* as a loud noise. It's not so much the loudness as the suddenness that is relevant here – a financial boom may burst upon us with as little warning as an ear-piercing one. In the economic sense *boom* first appears in the 1870s; within twenty years, presumably simply because it tripped off the tongue, someone had paired it with *bust* to describe a cycle in which the period of prosperity is followed by a crash.

brand

Early meanings of *brand* are to do with burning, as in a burning torch or the hot iron used to mark an animal with a symbol of ownership. From this also comes *firebrand*, which can mean a hot-headed, passionate person, as well as a piece of burning wood.

The idea of a *brand* as a trademark goes back to the eighteenth century, when manufacturers began to label all sorts of goods from timber to wine in a unique way (not necessarily by burning) to distinguish them from similar goods produced by someone else. From meaning specifically the mark, the word came to apply to the goods so branded, so that since the nineteenth century we have been able to talk about one *brand* of food or drink or tool being superior to another. As marketing became more sophisticated in the twentieth century we developed the concepts of *brand names*, *brand awareness*, *brand management* and *brand loyalty*.

It's only in the twenty-first century that a person or his or her output has come to be considered a *brand*: one now reads about *publishing brands* such as *Harry Potter* or *Fifty Shades of Grey* (series that the marketers can and do flog the hell out of). The many adaptations, sequels and re-imaginings of *Pride and Prejudice*, *Emma* et al have also led some journalists to write about the *Jane Austen brand*, although the lady would surely turn in her grave if she knew.

budget

When the British Chancellor of the Exchequer (the chief finance minister) leaves his official residence, Number Eleven Downing Street, to present his latest *budget* to the House of Commons, he traditionally poses for the media by holding up a red briefcase; this contains the hitherto confidential papers whose contents he is about to announce. The gesture may or may not be an indication that he understands what the word originally meant.

In fact, the first *budget* was not so much a briefcase as a leather pouch or wallet, a sense that was current in the fifteenth century and remained so well into the nineteenth. At the same time, it came to mean the contents of such a wallet or the contents of anything else, literally or figuratively: inviting someone to *open their budget* meant 'tell me what's on your mind'; and the *XXX Budget* could also be the name of a periodical, on a par with, say, the *Informer* or the *Bulletin*, suggesting that it contained *a budget of news*.

So how did the word come to be applied to the financial plans of the Chancellor of the Exchequer? As a result of an insult to the then First Lord of the Treasury Robert Walpole in 1733.

In addition to introducing highly unpopular tax reforms to Parliament, Walpole defended them in a pamphlet called *A letter from a Member of Parliament to his friends in the country, concerning the duties on wine and tobacco.* This prompted a satirical response from one of his fiercest opponents, William Pulteney, who produced the even more snappily titled *The Budget Opened. Or, An answer to a pamphlet. Intitled, a letter from a Member of Parliament to his friends in the country, concerning the duties on wine and tobacco.* 'The Mountain is deliver'd,' fumed Pulteney. 'The grand Mystery, which was long deemed too sacred for the unhallow'd Eyes of the People, is reveal'd ... The Budget is opened and our State Emperick hath dispensed his Packets by his Zany Couriers through all Parts of the Kingdom.' An Emperick was a quack doctor, and Pulteney meant, of course, that Walpole's shady secrets were now exposed to the scrutiny of all.

Walpole rode out this particular storm and Parliament took a fancy to the term *budget.* In the 1780s the *Annual Register*, summing up the year's events, reported that 'Mr Pitt opened the national accounts for the present year, or what is generally termed the Budget'; by the end of the century the word was being used without irony or explanation. From Westminster it soon spread to financial ministers across the world, and to the finances of businesses, households and individuals – *the company budget, the family budget, my holiday budget.*

By the middle of the twentieth century it had also acquired the nuance of *restricted* finances: thus *on a*

budget now means with limited money to spend, and
budget travel means you don't have to save up all year
in order to afford a holiday, though you may not be
guaranteed a seat on the PLANE.

Returning briefly to the Exchequer, a *cheque* (or
check) in the banking sense originally meant the
counterfoil of a bill of exchange or a request to pay
– the bit that the payer retained as evidence of how
much had been paid and to whom – and then became
the bill itself. The earliest *cheques* were associated
with *Exchequer* bills, and the Exchequer is a concept
dating back to Norman times, hence the French
spelling.

cabinet

Just as a BOARD was once the table around which
a group of directors sat, so a *cabinet* was a small
room in which a monarch's senior advisors met. This
sense of the word is older than you might think: the
diarist Walter Yonge recorded in 1625 that the newly
acceded Charles I 'made choice of six of the nobility
for his Council of the Cabinet' and within twenty
years, within the same reign, we find *cabinet* on its
own – without the 'Council of' – used in the sense in
which we use it in politics today.

In terms of word origin, *cabinet* is a diminutive of *cabin* and, before it had any political application, meant either a hut, or a garden summerhouse, or a small and private room, often with the implication that secrets were discussed there or intimate business carried out. The idea that it was a safe place also led to its being used for a case in which jewels and other valuables could be kept, and from that in turn evolved the concept of a cabinet in which precious and possibly fragile things could be displayed, either in a museum or in the home. So the safety remains, but not the secrecy. Whether that is true of a political cabinet is another matter.

cataract

The Ancient Greek and Latin ancestors of this word meant one of the things that *cataract* means in English today – a powerful waterfall. Some versions of the biblical book of Genesis, relating the story of Noah and the flood, refer to the *cataracts of Heaven* opening; the King James version has 'the windows of heaven', but clearly both mean 'flood gates' – once you open them, the previously controlled water bursts forth.

A drier version of a similar concept leads to the meaning of 'portcullis' – you do away with the water but still release a mechanism and in this case a gate slams down to block the castle entranceway. This is believed to be where the modern medical sense comes from: in the eye, a *cataract* is a condition whereby the lens becomes opaque, leading to impaired vision but not usually to total blindness. A portcullis in front of the eye would have much the same effect.

crunch

Until very recently, most of us would have thought that *crunch* was the noise we made when we ate a raw carrot, walked along a gravel path or possibly reversed our car into someone else's. Winston Churchill, in the run-up to the Second World War and referring to the situation in Europe, seems to have been the first person to use the word in the sense of a climax, a moment of confrontation, as in *when it comes to the crunch*.

Number-crunching, churning out large quantities of figures or other data without giving them much thought, is first heard of in the 1960s, perhaps coined because of the noise the calculating machine made. Then, of course, came the *credit crunch*, a period of economic crisis when it becomes difficult to borrow money, with the implication that financial institutions are collapsing noisily about our ears.

Like *number-crunching, credit crunch* was first recorded in the 1960s, but world finances recovered sufficiently for the term not to pass into common use. For a year or more after the global financial crisis of 2008, journalists were writing of the 'so-called credit crunch' or simply putting the words in inverted commas. It's a sad sign of the times that nobody does that any more – we all understand only too well what it means.

deadline

This is a slightly gruesome one. It was originally a literal *line* – drawn round a military prison. Any would-be escapee who crossed the line was liable to be shot. In this use *deadline* dates back to the American Civil War of the 1860s. By the 1920s it had been adopted into the modern sense of the time by which a journalist's copy must be filed, a college essay handed in or an application submitted. These days you aren't actually shot if you miss a deadline, but you could very well have blown your chances.

ether

Back in the day, *ether* or, more poetically, *aether*, was the pure upper air, outside the Earth's atmosphere. The Ancient Greeks divided the known world into four elements – water, air, earth and fire – and considered aether the fifth element: it circulated through the heavens, and the celestial bodies were composed of it. This concept persisted into the Middle Ages, when alchemists named a similar phenomenon *quintessence* or 'fifth essence'. Then in the eighteenth and nineteenth centuries aether became involved in all sorts of embryonic scientific theories, being regarded, among other things, as the medium through which light travelled.

Odd, then, that it should have become the name of a compound best known as an anaesthetic. For that we have to thank an eighteenth-century German chemist named August Sigmund Frobenius, who studied the properties of a liquid called sweet oil of vitriol, known to have some medicinal uses. He discovered, among other things, that 'a little of it poured on the Surface of the Hand affects it with a Sense of Cold equal to that from the Contact of Snow'. Frobenius called this liquid *Spiritus Vini Aethereus* – ethereal spirit of wine. Today chemists refer to it as diethyl ether or $C_2H_2OC_2H_5$, but it remains simply *ether* to the rest of us.

It's from the age-old idea that all sorts of things could travel through the *aether* that we get the modern concept of a vague place through which DIGITAL information travels and in which emails get lost. Even this isn't very modern, though: voices and information have been being sent out *into the ether* since the early days of radio, almost a century ago.

floss

Here's a surprising fact: there's a character in James Joyce's *Ulysses* who carries *dental floss* around in his waistcoat pocket. The text says that he 'twanged it smartly between two and two of his resonant unwashed teeth', so presumably other aspects of his oral hygiene left something to be desired.

The concept of *flossing* has been around since the early nineteenth century and the fact that *dental floss* was originally made of silk explains its name. The primary meaning of *floss* is the rough silk surrounding the cocoon of a silkworm. This, and similar fibres from cotton and other plants, can be spun into fine filaments such as those we pull between our teeth. Nowadays dental floss is generally synthetic, though *embroidery floss* may still be made from silk.

issue

Not obvious at first glance, this is related to *exit*,
from the Latin and Old French for 'flowing out'. So
water might *issue* from a floodgate, an army *issue*
forth from its headquarters or blood *issue* from a
wound. From this root many meanings have sprouted.
The idea that children *issue* from their parents gave
the word the meaning of 'offspring', often in a legal
context: Mark Antony in Shakespeare's *Julius Caesar*
talks of 'bequeathing ... a rich legacy unto their issue'.
By this time – the late sixteenth century – it had also
come to mean an outcome, a result or the crux of a
matter, hence *the point at issue*, the matter you are
debating, or *to take issue*, to differ, to take someone up
on a statement with which you disagree.

All these senses were current, in and out of the
law courts, for several hundred years before another
modern one came along: an *issue* of postage stamps
or bank notes, from about the 1830s, meant those
that were put out at the same time and had the same
denomination, colour and so forth. By extension, an
issue of a periodical meant all those copies produced
and distributed on a certain date and with the same
design and content.

But perhaps the most common modern meaning
evolves from *the point at issue*. Sometime in the
1980s, possibly when more people than ever before
were going into therapy with a view to sorting out

their problems, accentuating the positive became the thing to do. Thus *issue* became the standard term for an emotional hurdle that needed to be overcome, just as anything difficult became *challenging*, helping you to gloss over the fact that you had any problems at all.

kettling

The German *Kesselschlacht* (literally 'cauldron battle') means a pincer movement, in which an attacking force approaches the enemy from two angles with a view to surrounding and isolating them. The Germans used the word to describe the tactics employed against them by the Russians in the Battle of Stalingrad in 1942–3 and also for the way they (the Germans) rounded up Jews in the Warsaw ghetto at about the same time.

It's likely that this has influenced the modern English use of *kettling*, a police method of controlling demonstrators by forcing them into a confined space and guarding the only exit. It has been suggested that both the concept and the name reached England from Germany in the 1980s, after British police observed how their German counterparts dealt with crowd control at sports matches. In addition to restricting movement, *kettling* carries the implication that what is enclosed could easily bubble up and boil over, as water does in a domestic kettle if you leave it on the heat too long.

loophole

The interesting thing about a literal *loophole* is that it was put there on purpose, whereas in figurative use it is almost bound to be an accident. Historically, a *loophole* was a gap in the wall of a fortification that someone inside could shoot through or simply keep watch from. In fact, the word is a bit of a tautology, as *loop* on its own would mean the same thing – it probably comes from a Dutch word meaning 'to peer' and is nothing to do with the sort of loop you make with wool in knitting or when turning a rope into a lasso.

A *loophole* in the sense of 'a means of escape, especially an ambiguity in the drafting of a law' is found as early as the seventeenth century, while the concept is as old as the Roman orator Cicero. Writing to his brother Quintus in 56 BC about the successful outcome of a trial, he refers to Quintus's concern lest he leave any 'loophole for abuse' to an unfriendly critic. The Latin is *vituperandi locum*, which means nothing more than 'place for abuse', but the early twentieth-century translator who called it a loophole clearly understood what Cicero had in mind.

nucleus

Nux is the Latin for 'nut' and *nucellus* is a little nut. That word still exists in botany to describe the tissue within a plant's ovule, which contains the embryo-sac. From this comes *nucleus*, which even in Ancient Rome meant a kernel or inner part. So it was logical that astronomers, who in the seventeenth century would have been writing up their findings in Latin, should adopt the word to mean the central part of a comet or nebula; and later that atomic scientists should use it for the core of an atom. Nowadays *nucleus* can be applied to the idea around which a theory is developed or a small group of people working within a larger organization. In fact, a nucleus can be part of almost anything – just as long as it's in the centre.

nutraceutical

A modern piece of jargon combining *nutrient* or *nutrition* and *pharmaceutical*, this refers to the

dietary supplements that are supposed to do us good
but which, by law, their manufacturers and marketers
aren't allowed to call medicines. A 2009 article in the
Guardian, headed 'Are probiotics really that good for
your health?', referred to the fact that 'a huge number
of us have been persuaded by advertisers that we
need our daily "nutraceutical" dose'. The piece was
illustrated by a photograph of those little pots of
yoghurt that we are told promote our 'beneficial gut
microflora' – what copywriters have been known to
call 'friendly bacteria'. At the time that article was
written, the word *nutraceutical* had been around
for twenty years, but it's noticeable that it appears
in inverted commas, as if to emphasize the 'pseudo'
element of the pseudoscience that many people feel is
behind this sort of nutritional advice.

Probiotic is a slightly older word, a combination
of *pro*, meaning forward or in favour of, and *biotic*,
relating to life. It was coined – as an obvious antonym
of *antibiotic* – in the 1950s, although it didn't move
out of the scientific journals into the wider world
until the 1980s. That may be because it wasn't
until the 1980s or so that the wider world became
remotely interested in the growth of microorganisms
in its own gut.

precariat

In 2013 Professor Guy Standing of the London School
of Oriental and African Studies published a book
called *The Precariat: The New Dangerous Class*. In it
he identified an emerging social class of dissatisfied
people, including many educated youngsters, 'living
bits-and-pieces lives, in and out of short-term jobs'
and 'divided into angry and bitter factions'. What
he was doing was taking the established word
proletariat and predicting a *precarious* future for
many of its members – and members of other classes
too. The word isn't yet in common usage but, if the
social trend it describes persists, it soon will be.

siren

In 1819, there appeared in the French publication
Annales de chimie et de physique ('Annals of chemistry
and physics') a paper by one Baron Charles Cagniard
de la Tour, entitled 'On the Siren, new acoustic
machine designed to measure the vibrations in the
air which constitute sound'. What the Baron had
produced was a circular copper box, about 10 cm
in diameter, rotating on an axis and with a hundred
holes cut in the top. Into this he pumped air or water
by means of a bellows and he noted that his device

produced different notes depending on how fast the box was rotating. All this was an improvement on the work of the Scottish scientist John Robison, who twenty years earlier had produced a less sophisticated contraption that could power some of the pipes in an organ.

De la Tour called his invention a *sirène* or siren and it was this name that was given later in the nineteenth century to the hooters, larger in size but similar in principle, that enabled ships and lighthouses to make others aware of their presence in fog. In due course there followed *air-raid sirens*, *fire-engine sirens* and other devices designed to emit loud noises by way of warning.

But the original Sirens weren't noisy mechanical devices, or even primitive musical instruments. They were monsters, part woman, part bird, in Greek mythology, who sang with great sweetness and lured sailors to their doom on the rocks. Their name came to be used to describe any tempting female who charmed a man away from the straight and narrow, not necessarily by singing to him. One of the characteristics of the mythological Sirens was their mermaid-like swimming ability and it seems that, in christening his ACOUSTIC device, Baron de la Tour ignored the destructiveness of the Sirens and the entrancing beauty of their song, and concentrated on a lesser attribute – their ability to function underwater.

smog

This word for *smoke* mixed with *fog* – a danger to
life and traffic in London in particular in the period
between the arrival of the Industrial Revolution
(late eighteenth century) and the implementation
of the Clean Air Act (1956) – was coined in 1905 by
Dr Henri de Voeux, in a paper delivered at a public
health conference, highlighting the problems of
urban pollution. London may have been cleaned up
by restrictions on the burning of coal, but *smog* is
still a hazard of cities such as Beijing, where traffic
emissions, dust from building works and so on clog
the atmosphere. The word is now used more loosely
to describe not necessarily a mixture of smoke and
fog, but any health-threatening level of 'particulate
matter' in the air.

tank

You might not think there was much connection
between the container of water in which you keep
tropical fish and the heavily armoured vehicle that
shares its name, but the latter does indeed derive
from the former. From the seventeenth century in
India, a *tank* has been a large storage container for
water, more like a reservoir than a fish bowl. The OED

has a nineteenth-century citation referring to a tank covering 72 acres – that's around 28 hectares or 40 soccer pitches. It would hold a lot of fish.

By the end of the seventeenth century *tank* was being applied to smaller containers, of the fish-keeping variety. When motor cars were invented and contained a receptacle for carrying fuel, that too became known as a tank.

But what about the armoured vehicles? Although inventors had been working on the idea for a hundred years before, *tanks* as we know them were developed during the First World War. An ex-soldier turned journalist called Ernest Swinton, appalled at the carnage he saw in the trenches in 1914, set his mind to finding a better way to defend the infantry against machine-gun attack. With the support of Winston Churchill, then First Lord of the Admiralty, a committee was established to look into Swinton's proposals and then put them into action. Commissioning and producing such a vehicle in wartime obviously had to be kept secret, so it needed a codename. The basic outline of the vehicle struck someone as looking like a water reservoir, so a *tank* the new secret weapon became – and has remained ever since.

Tank has also produced a few interesting derivatives. In slang usage, *to be tanked up* means 'to have drunk enough to fill a tank' – a sense that must refer to the water tank or fish tank, as it predates the invention of the armoured vehicle. From the late twentieth century, we have the apparently unexplained meaning from competitive sport of 'to throw a match away, to lose deliberately' and hence, of stocks and shares or a film at the box office, 'to fail spectacularly'. More recently still, in the subgenre of electronic games known as MMORPG (Massively Multiplayer Online Role-Playing Games), a *tank* is a character that absorbs damage aimed at another without being badly damaged itself. For something that started out as a secret codename, it has spread its influence pretty widely.

transistor

At its simplest, this is a device that largely replaced the valve in an electronic circuit because it was smaller, more reliable and worked at a lower voltage, with much less output of heat. Invention of the name is credited to the American engineer John R. Pierce, who was supervising the development of the technology at Bell Laboratories in the 1940s:

> [The device] was supposed to be the dual
> of the vacuum tube. The vacuum tube had

transconductance, so the transistor would have 'transresistance'. And the name should fit in with the names of other devices, such as varistor and thermistor ... I suggested the name 'transistor'.

Assuming you have little idea what *transconductance, transresistance, varistor* and *thermistor* mean, it's perhaps easier to remember that a transistor *transfers* electric signals across a *resistor*.

Interestingly, for all the technical explanations about semiconductors and electrodes, the key thing about a transistor – as far as the general public was concerned – was its size. The word is first recorded in 1948; by 1958 the *Spectator* was writing about 'the new miniature transistor radios', which meant 'radios operated by a transistor device'. Within another decade 'miniature' in that expression would have been considered superfluous, because no one gave a thought to the technology: the point of a *transistor radio* was that it was small and portable.

workaholic

The adjective *alcoholic*, meaning 'containing alcohol', dates back to the eighteenth century; the noun meaning 'a person who is addicted to alcohol' doesn't appear until the middle of the nineteenth – surprisingly late, considering how much they put away in Regency times a few decades earlier. But although addiction to opium and its derivatives also goes back into the mists of time, it wasn't until the mid-twentieth century that people started jokingly describing themselves as being addicted to other, less blatantly harmful things. In 1947 the *Toronto Daily Star* referred satirically to an organization called Workaholics Synonymous, aimed at helping those 'cursed with an unconquerable craving for work'. There's no etymological justification for *workaholic*, because the *-holic* part of *alcoholic* is nothing to do with addiction; *workaholic* is what is called a nonce word, made up to suit a given occasion. Nevertheless, *tobaccoholic*, *sugarholic*, *chocoholic*, *shopaholic* and others soon followed.

Addiction to chocolate can be a serious business. It's been suggested that worried chocoholics should try a *dechox*, but it remains to be seen if this will catch on.

CHAPTER SIX

Fashion Tips

From the kitten heel to the turtle neck,
this is a brief look at why we call some
of our garments by such strange names.

basque

What we now think of as a *basque* is a woman's all-in-one undergarment, close-fitting but lacking the bones or wiring that would make it a corset; a *basque waistline* on a dress dips into a V shape at the front, elongating the torso and flattering the waist. In the nineteenth century, however, a *basque* was more like a long bodice or a short jacket – in 1860 the teenaged heroine of Miriam Coles Harris's Gothic novel *Rutledge* was able to put her hands in the pockets of hers, so it presumably wasn't the lacy item sold under that name today.

But before all this a *basque* was a male garment – an extension of a doublet or waistcoat. The style and the name were adopted by the French in about the seventeenth century, presumably because they had seen it in the Basque Country. One extraordinary image, from a book of French national costumes published in 1939, shows a Basque man wearing a huge crown of flowers and a close-fitting jacket whose 'skirt' extends over an oblong frame. From the hem of the jacket hangs a knee-length lace skirt bedecked with large bows. It is, to say the least, an unusual look and you can see why it went out of fashion. The real question is why it should ever have been in fashion in the first place.

bolero

This was originally a Spanish dance, first noted in Britain in the 1780s and adopted as the title of a piece for ballet by the French composer Maurice Ravel. A great success at its premiere in 1928, Ravel's *Boléro* reached a new generation when it helped the ice dancers Jayne Torvill and Christopher Dean to win a gold medal at the 1984 Winter Olympics.

However, neither Torvill nor Dean *wore* a bolero. It's a short jacket that doesn't reach the waist and doesn't fasten up the front. Originally (in Spain) worn by men when they were performing the dance of the same name, it's not unlike the jackets worn by bullfighters. A bolero is now more likely to be worn by women, over a blouse or dress, and covers little more than the shoulders and upper arms. Adopting the name of the dance for the jacket was presumably a marketing decision, for there have been many variations on the same theme: the OED quotes this report on 1892 fashions from the *Daily News*:

> The Zouave is as great a favourite as it has been for some seasons, and though it varies in form – being sometimes a bolero, sometimes a toreador, and sometimes a cross between an Eton jacket and a Zouave.

I trust this clears up any remaining confusion.

kitten heel

Low, tapering heels on a woman's shoe, *kittens* aren't as overtly sexy as STILETTOS and were once marketed as 'training heels'. Considered suitable for a first foray into 'heels' for young teenage girls, they became all the rage in the 1950s when they were adopted by that most stylish of screen stars, Audrey Hepburn. And why kitten? Because they were *kittenish* – playful and innocent, but perhaps with the promise of something less chaste to come.

mini

The word *miniature* derives from Italian and the fact that it resembles *minimum* and other words to do with smallness is a coincidence: its origins lie in the Latin *miniatus*, which means stained red and was applied to a pigment used to decorate medieval manuscripts. From this it transferred to the decorations themselves, which it just so happened tended to be small. In English *miniature* was originally a noun, meaning – from the sixteenth century – a very small portrait, and the derived adjective took on its modern meaning of 'on a small scale, smaller in size than the original'. Hence the various *minis* that found their way into the language in the twentieth century: there was a *minimeter* for measuring tiny distances; an Art Deco *minipiano* otherwise known as the 'Pianette'; and, of course, come 1959, the *Mini Minor* car and, a few years later, the *miniskirt*, thanks respectively to the British Motor Corporation and Alec Issigonis, and to designers André Courrèges and Mary Quant.

Skirts as short as the 1960s minis were always likely to produce a backlash, so that by the end of that decade there was not only a *maxi skirt* (generally ankle- or floor-length) but also a *midi*, somewhere between the two at around mid-calf.

See also MINIBUS.

stiletto

This Italian word meaning 'little dagger' derives from the Latin *stilus*, the pointed instrument the Romans used for writing on wax TABLETS. It's connected with *style*, and also with the *stylus* used to play gramophone records.

Stiletto meaning dagger is first found in English in the early seventeenth century as the weapon of choice for desperados marauding the streets of Venice. It was still current in 1953, when the victim in Josephine Tey's thriller *The Man in the Queue* is stabbed with 'a thin, exceedingly sharp stiletto ...' In those days, when no one seems to have been very sensitive to racial stereotyping, this enables the detective to assume that the murderer is of Latin origin: it's not a weapon a 'thorough Englishman' would have used. But in that very year, an American publication was writing about the new fashion in Italian footwear, 'the slender fabric shoe, poised on a slim dagger of a heel'. The word *stiletto* had taken on a new meaning, and thorough Englishwomen (and English speakers the world over) were happy to embrace it.

thong

The word *thong* has been around for over a thousand years in the sense of 'a narrow strip of leather serving as a cord, a shoelace or the like'. From that, by the sixteenth century, it had come to mean a leather whip, used either for punishing people or for encouraging horses to move along. In due course Australians and Americans adopted it to mean what the British call a *flip-flop* – a sandal consisting of little more than a sole and a narrow strap designed to slide between the big and second toes.

This sort of thong arrived in the 1950s, but was superseded in the 1970s by an innovation in swimwear designed by Rudi Gernreich, an Austrian-born American who spent most of his career coming up with designs that some described as avant-garde and others considered downright shocking. When he produced a swimsuit with nothing below the waist at the back but a strip of material passing between the buttocks, he chose to call it a *thong* and the name also came to be used for lingerie of a similar design.

Ten years earlier, Gernreich had designed the *monokini*, a woman's one-piece swimsuit that ended just above the waist, leaving the breasts exposed. The name, of course, is a play on *bikini*: *mono* comes from the Greek for 'one' and in many words (*biplane*, *bipolar*, *biped*) bi- means 'two'. Not in *bikini*, though, despite the fact that the garment is a 'two-piece'. *Bikini* is the name of a group of islands in the Pacific and the word's origins lie in a local language. My guess is that Gernreich knew this perfectly well and coined the inaccurate *monokini* for the fun of it. He seems to have been that sort of guy.

turtle neck

The OED dates this fashion style to the 1890s and defines it precisely as a 'close-fitting roll or band collar, now usually one intermediate in height between a crew-neck and a polo-neck'. Despite an appealing story suggesting that an eccentric Swedish inventor designed a long-necked sweater to keep his pet turtles warm when he took them for walks, it's more likely that someone thought that the way the wearer's head appeared through a turtle-neck sweater looked like the way a real turtle's head pops in and out of its shell. Or that the folds or rolls of the collar itself resembled the ones in the neck of those long-lived and crinkly reptiles.

For what it's worth, a *polo neck* is so called because it looks like the shirts worn by polo players, and the lower *crew neck* is a style favoured by oarsmen. As for the hairstyle known as the *crew cut*, it was apparently first adopted by boat crews at Harvard and Yale. The term emerged in the 1930s and 1940s, so perhaps in the competitive world of 'The Race' between those two universities it was an early aerodynamic variation on the cyclists' idea that shaving your legs allows you to go faster.

yoke

The concept of joining two animals together and hooking them up to a plough has been around since agriculture was invented, and the word *yoke*, to signify either the action or the device that was used to perform it, dates back a thousand years. Its origin can be traced to words for *to join* in a number of languages. Because similar devices were sometimes put round the necks of conquered enemies, the word came to mean a state of submission or servitude, as in 'south-eastern Europe was under the yoke of the Ottoman Empire', and unhappy spouses were known to refer to 'the yoke of matrimony'.

But in the fashion sense, *yoke* goes back to the early, uncomplaining meaning. It was originally the part of a garment made to fit the shoulders (or the hips, if it was a skirt or pair of trousers), to which the rest was attached. The fact that on a dress or blouse the yoke was often of a different material, such as lace, or was more decorated than the rest of the garment, has distracted us from the fact that it was originally designed to join the other parts together.

zip

The oldest meaning of *zip* dates to the late nineteenth century and describes the sound made by mosquitoes or speeding bullets (for a similar speedy-sounding concept, see ZOOM). By the beginning of the twentieth it was being used figuratively to mean zest or energy. A combination of these things may be what the 1920s inventors of the *zip, zipper* or *zip fastener* had in mind. A similar device had been patented in the 1850s by Elias Howe, the pioneering sewing-machine manufacturer, who called it an 'Automatic, Continuous Clothing Closure' – not exactly a marketing department's dream. Other people had worked on the idea in the interim, but it was the B. F. Goodrich Company, inserting these fasteners into their new range of galoshes in the 1920s, that found the name that would sell.

CHAPTER SEVEN

A Splash of Colour

Much of our colour imagery is easy to explain: black and white equate to darkness and light, gold and silver indicate richness. Straightforward enough. This short chapter looks at some of the less self-evident links and how our most familiar colours became involved with politics, cowardice and melancholy.

blue

No one seems to be sure why *blue* was chosen as the colour of sorrowfulness. The earliest citation is dated 1450 and describes a heart being *black and blue* at the death of a friend, which suggests, touchingly, that the heart was bruised. But there is also a mischievous creature known as a *blue devil*, who from the seventeenth century was blamed for making people miserable by giving them *a fit of the blue devils*. Those same *blue devils*, by the late eighteenth century, were sent to plague drunkards, a hundred years before they started seeing pink elephants.

It was also in the eighteenth century that people starting suffering from *the blues*, although it isn't clear whether or not this was originally an abbreviation of *blue devils*. But it is highly likely that these were the *blues* that, in the late nineteenth century, gave their name to a certain type of melancholy music that had originated among the black population of the American South.

green

Figurative meanings of *green* go back a long way, and refer to freshness, innocence or naivety – the qualities of spring and, by extension, of youth. Shakespeare has

Cleopatra refer to 'my salad days, when I was green in judgement', meaning the time when she preferred Caesar to Antony, with the clear implication that she is wiser now. Anyone who knows the play *Antony and Cleopatra* will have their own opinion on that, but let us not digress …

It seems to be Shakespeare, too, who popularized the idea of being *green with envy*: Portia in *The Merchant of Venice* refers to *green-ey'd jealousy* and Iago warns Othello against *the green-ey'd monster*. Yet green has been seen as the colour of illness, and in particular biliousness, for much longer than that. A sickly complexion could be caused by envy but could also be the result of unrequited love: the Greek poet Sappho, writing in the sixth century BC, has a jealous lover refer to herself as *greener than the greenest grass* and on the verge of death.

Green in the environmental sense takes us back to the more positive idea of fresh growth and healthy plant life. In 1971 a boat named *Greenpeace* sailed from Vancouver into the Arctic Ocean as a protest against the planned testing of a nuclear bomb there. The name was chosen by one of the activists, Bill Darnell, as linking the concerns of ecologists and the peace movement. A sympathetic journalist, Bob Hunter, wrote in the *Vancouver Sun*, 'All along I have believed that ecology is a bridge of green, spanning not only the generation gap but the gap between workers and students, left and right, rich and poor.' Clearly both Darnell and Hunter saw green as the colour that the Earth should be – and that it would cease to be if the testing of nuclear bombs was allowed to continue. The Greenpeace organization was taking its first steps.

The first person to be elected to a national parliament as a member of a Green Party was Daniel Brélaz; this was in Switzerland in 1971. Green Parties were soon to be found all over Europe, notably in Germany, where the Grüne Aktion Zukunft (Green Action for the Future) was one of the forerunners of that country's present Green Alliance. The UK's Ecology Party, founded in 1975, changed its name to the Green Party in 1985, by which time Green Parties also existed in the USA and Canada. The word is now universally recognized as being synonymous with 'ecologically friendly' and 'concerned with the future of the planet'. But all is not sweetness and harmony with greenness: it's still the colour you turn when you feel envious or seasick.

red

During the French Revolution (1789–99), *red* was the colour not of socialism or communism but of revolt. It apparently alludes to the blood shed by 'the workers' in their struggle against an oppressive regime; the *red bonnet* worn by many revolutionaries became a powerful symbol. A later generation of French revolutionaries raised a *red flag* during the Paris Uprising of 1832 (against King Louis-Philippe), as had protesting miners during the Merthyr rebellion in South Wales the previous year. And when in 1848 the French succeeded in overthrowing Louis-Philippe, there was a move to replace the Tricolour flag with a red one. The poet and politician Alphonse de Lamartine, foreign minister at the time, rejected this appeal on the grounds that a red flag was (symbolically) soaked in the blood of French citizens.

All this was, you might say, politically left of centre. Certainly the red flag, bloodshed and the activities of socialists and others concerned with workers' rights became inextricably linked in the minds of those whose interests were more conservative.

It got worse – as far as the traditionalists were concerned, that is. In 1889, the Irishman Jim Connell's lyrics for what became the socialist anthem, 'The Red Flag', continued to lay emphasis on bloodshed:

> The people's flag is deepest red,
> It shrouded oft our martyr'd dead
> And ere their limbs grew stiff and cold,
> Their hearts' blood dyed its ev'ry fold.

Then in 1923, the newly formed Soviet Union adopted a red flag adorned with the hammer and sickle (symbols respectively of urban and rural workers) and retained it until the Union was dissolved in 1991. *Red* came firmly to mean *communist*, particularly for those driven by anti-Russian paranoia at the height of the Cold War, who couldn't go to sleep at night without checking that there were no *reds under the bed*.

If you dilute the colour red with white, of course, you get *pink* and as early as the 1920s someone whose views were leftish but not hard line was being described as *pink* or, derogatorily, a *pinko*.

Red Square in Moscow, by the way, has been so called since the seventeenth century. The Russian word *krasnaya* means both *red* and *beautiful*, so the name has no political significance.

yellow

As with BLUE and melancholy, there's doubt and speculation about why *yellow* came to be associated with cowardice. *Yellow belly* is recorded in British English in the eighteenth century as a type of frog and also as a nickname for the people of the Fens – whether from their unhealthy complexion or because they lived in the same sort of damp conditions as the frog isn't clear. Either way, there's no reason to suppose that this crossed the Atlantic, and certainly *yellow belly* and *yellow* as terms for cowardice originated in American English. By 1850 *yellow belly* was 'a name given by Western hunters and soldiers to the Mexicans', presumably a not exactly politically correct allusion to the colour of their skin. And just as British English adopted all sorts of abusive expressions concerning the Dutch and the French (think *double Dutch* and *French leave*) when the various countries were at war, so the meaning of *yellow belly* may have evolved to be insulting to an enemy, even one who wasn't a Mexican; *yellow* on its own was in use only a few years later. Both terms soon lost the racial slur and became a general term of abuse for any cowardly or contemptible person, particularly in a Western movie.

A coward may also be described as *lily-livered*, which means his liver is white – presumably a bad thing. Towards the end of Shakespeare's *Macbeth*, a terrified servant comes to report to his master that a force of 10,000 soldiers is approaching the castle. Macbeth replies:

Go, prick thy face, and over-red thy fear
Thou lily-liver'd boy ...
        Those linen cheeks of thine
Are counsellors to fear.

In other words, pallor is cowardly and will frighten others too. Painting it over with blood will make you look braver. There is perhaps a touch of desperation about this advice: I suggest that smearing your face with blood is not the best way to disguise your nervousness at an interview or on a first date.

Acknowledgements

Many thanks to the various friends who suggested words to be included, notably Anne and Derek, Carol, Dave and Sheila, Elaine, Ros and Sam, and Sheena. Thanks and love also to Rebecca and to everyone at Michael O'Mara Books, especially George Maudsley, for making the book happen.

Bibliography

Bierce, Ambrose *The Devil's Dictionary* (first published 1911; reissued by The Folio Society, 2003)

Flavell, Linda and Roger *Dictionary of Word Origins* (Kyle Cathie, 1993, revised 2008)

Flavell, Linda and Roger *Dictionary of English Down the Ages* (Kyle Cathie, 1999, revised 2005)

Green, Jonathon *Slang Dictionary* (Chambers, 2008)

McDonald, Fred *The Penguin Book of Word Histories* (Penguin, 2010)

The OED online, which I access courtesy of Westminster Libraries, was my first port of call to establish meanings and dates of first recorded uses. I've also consulted *The Chambers Dictionary, The Collins English Dictionary* and *The Oxford English Reference Dictionary*.

Research for a book like this involves much following of links and hopes (often fulfilled) of serendipitous discoveries. Specific information on the following words came from these sites:

Advertorial: **www.write.co.nz**

Basque: **world4.eu/traditional-french-national-costumes/#Related_books** (do go to this page and have a look at the weird costume I have attempted to describe)

Biopic: **www.filmreference.com**

Budget: **historyofparliamentblog.wordpress.com**

Caravan: **https://eugenebyrne.wordpress.com**

Cartoon: **www.punch.co.uk**

Cookie: **cookiecontroller.com**

Cougar: **www.defenders.org** *and* **www.thestar.com.my/story/**

Ether: **rstl.royalsocietypublishing.org**

Express: **www.seat61.com**

Juggernaut: **www.historyinthemargins.com**

Kettling: **flesl.net/**

Muzak: **news.google.com/newspapers**

Patience/solitaire: **www.davpar.eu/**

Podcast: **www.theguardian.com/media/2004/feb/12/**

Siren: **books.google.co.uk/books**

Spam: **www.spam.com**

Stall: **spartacus-educational.com/Jsala.htm**

Tank: **www.firstworldwar.com/weaponry/tanks.htm**

Index

Words in **bold** are main entries.

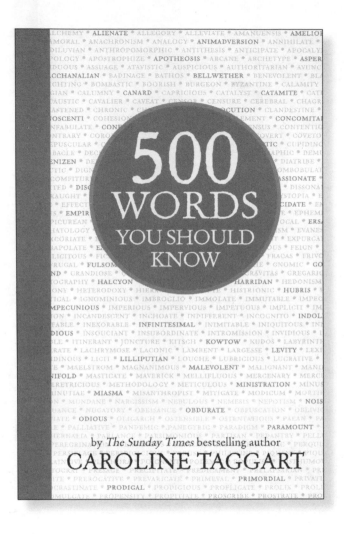

by *The Sunday Times* bestselling author
CAROLINE TAGGART

500 Words You Should Know

978-1-78243-294-4

£9.99